YOUNG STUDENTS
Learning
Library®

VOLUME 8

Elgar, Edward William —
Flightless Birds

NEWFIELD
PUBLICATIONS
SHELTON, CONNECTICUT

CREDITS

Page 900 Dennis Gilbert; 901 National Gallery of Art, Washington, DC; 902 Armando Curcio Editore (top left); National Portrait Gallery (bottom); 903 Camera Press; 906 Hulton Picture Company; 907 Armando Curcio Editore; 909 British Museum; 910 Michael Holford (top left); 920 Dennis Gilbert (top); Michael Holford (bottom); 921 Dennis Gilbert; 922 Dennis Gilbert; 923 British Museum; 927 Fotomas Index (top); Mary Evans (bottom); 928 University of Leeds; 929 Mansell Collection; 930 British Library; 935 Satour; 937 ZEFA; 938 Armando Curcio Editore; 939 National Gallery of Art, Washington, DC; 941 Ronald Sheriday; 946 ZEFA; 947 Armando Curcio Editore; 948 Imperial War Museum; 949 ZEFA; 950 Biofotos; 951 ZEFA; 953 Imitor; 954 Royal College of Surgeons/Rainbird; 955 Imitor; 957 Michael Holford (top); Colour Centre Slides Ltd (bottom); 958 British Library; 961 Mansell Collection; 962 Popperfoto (top); NASA (bottom); 964 Hulton Picture Company (top left); Armando Curcio Editore (bottom left); Kramarsky Trust (bottom right); 965 Mary Evans Picture Library/Harry Price Collection, University of London; 970 Cannon (UK) Ltd; 971 Sonia Halliday/Bibliotheque Nationale, Paris; 972 Dr. Pat Morris; 975 Robert Harding Assoc; 979 Hulton Picture Company; 982 Kyoto Costume Institute; 983 Armando Curcio Editore (top left); Paul Forrester (middle); Hulton Picture Library (bottom left); 985 Peter Newark Pictures; 988 F.B.I.; 994 Courtaulds; 999 Finnish Tourist Board; 1001 Fire Chief Robert Groshen 1002 ZEFA; 1003 ZEFA (bottom); 1011 Biofotos; 1015 State of New Hampshire (top); New Hampshire Office of Vacation Travel (bottom) 1016 ZEFA; 1018 V & A Museum; 1019 ZEFA.

Young Students Learning Library and Newfield Publications are federally registered trademarks of Newfield Publications, Inc.

Copyright © 1994 by Newfield Publications, Inc.; 1974, 1972 by Funk & Wagnalls, Inc. & Newfield Publications, Inc.

Maps containing the appropriate Donnelley indication are copyright © 1994 by R.R. Donnelley and Sons Company. This product contains proprietart property of R.R. Donnelley & Sons Company.

Unauthorized use, including copying, of this product is expressly prohibited.

Printed in the U.S.A.

ISBN 0-8374-9815-5

CONTENTS

▲ Blythburgh church, in Suffolk, ENGLAND, was built in the Middle Ages with money made from the wool trade.

ELGAR, EDWARD WILLIAM (1857–1934)

Probably the best-known British classical music of this century was written by Edward Elgar. He is acknowledged as the greatest British composer since Henry Purcell in the 17th century.

Elgar was born near Worcester, in the English midlands close to the border with Wales. His father kept a music store, but Edward had no formal musical training. As a young man, he rode a bicycle for miles through the green hills of the countryside around his home. Later, he wrote music that reflected some of the beauty of the landscape he loved.

Elgar settled in London. He married and worked as a teacher. His music first attracted praise in Germany, but it was not long before he was famous in Britain. He was given a knighthood in 1904. Elgar's major works include the oratorio (religious choral work) "The Dream of Gerontius"; two concertos for violin and cello; and the "Enigma Variations" (in which the tune, or theme, is varied to describe the characters of several of the composer's friends). Among Elgar's most popular compositions are the marches called "Pomp and Circumstance." These were composed for the coronation of King Edward VII in 1902, and from them comes the patriotic British song, "Land of Hope and Glory."

▶▶▶▶ **FIND OUT MORE** ◀◀◀◀
Composer; Music

 **EL GRECO (about 1541–1614)**

One of the great artists of Spain was a foreigner with a name so hard to pronounce that he was known as "the Greek." Even today, we remember that great painter, Doménikos Theotokópoulos, by his nickname in Spanish—El Greco.

His early training as an artist on the island of Crete was in the Byzantine style, which survives today in the Eastern Orthodox churches. El Greco went to Italy to study while in his twenties. He worked under the great artist Titian in Venice, and then went on to Rome to study the work of the masters Raphael and Michelangelo.

The artist then traveled to Spain where he settled in the city of Toledo. Over the next 36 years, he painted landscapes, portraits, pictures of saints, and religious scenes.

The person riding horseback pictured here is Saint Martin, dividing his cloak in two to give half to a beggar. According to the legend, the beggar later turned out to be Jesus Christ. The beggar does not look bent down or defeated. Saint Martin looks concerned about the shivering beggar.

Can you see the Byzantine way of painting? Do you see the lack of depth, or *perspective,* for instance? The artist puts figures up in the foreground in front of a very low horizon. But other features of El Greco's paintings are entirely his own creation. His people have a strange, mystical look, as if from another world. His figures and landscapes are often lengthened and twisted. His colors combine brilliant splashes of light and somber shadows. And they almost seem to move. To El Greco, movement was all important.

Many of El Greco's works decorated the chapels and monasteries of Toledo, Spain. He was also an architect and sculptor, and created altarpieces. But when he died, El Greco was almost forgotten. His style of painting went out of fashion. French painters, particularly Paul Cézanne, rediscovered him 250 years later. Although El Greco had worked years earlier, his paintings expressed feelings in ways that modern artists were trying to achieve in their work.

▶▶▶▶ **FIND OUT MORE** ◀◀◀◀
Art History; Painting

▲ **Sir Edward Elgar, British composer.**

▲ *Saint Martin and the Beggar* **by El Greco, National Gallery of Art, Washington, D.C., Widener Collection.**

Although George Eliot left school when she was 16, she was one of the most learned women of her day. She could read Latin, Greek, French, Italian, German, and Hebrew, and was also a talented pianist.

▲ George Eliot, British novelist.

▲ T.S. Eliot, a major 20th-century writer, best known for his poetry.

ELIOT, GEORGE (1819–1880)

The books written by George Eliot were the work not of a man, but of a woman. Her name was Mary Ann (or Marian) Evans. George Eliot was a *pen name* (pseudonym). Under that name, she wrote some of the best novels in the English language.

Mary Ann Evans was born in Warwickshire, England, and she was brought up in the countryside. She kept house for her father until he died in 1849, but she was interested in writing and new ideas. She moved to London and began working as an editor on a magazine. Through her magazine work and her interest in literature, she met many of the leading writers and thinkers of the day, such as Thomas Carlyle and John Stuart Mill. With one of these new friends, George Henry Lewes, she began a lifelong relationship, and he encouraged her to write novels.

In those days it was not easy for a woman to be accepted as a serious writer. So Mary Ann Evans took the pen name of George Eliot. The first of her many novels was *Adam Bede* (1859), which was highly praised. Among her other novels, all of which skillfully depict the country people she knew so well, are *The Mill on the Floss, Silas Marner,* and *Middlemarch.* Her books are admired for their realism, shrewd characterization, and strong moral feeling.

After George Henry Lewes died, in 1878, she was greatly distressed and shut herself away from society. In the spring of 1880, she married longtime friend John Walter Cross, but she died a few months later.

ELIOT, T. S. (1888–1965)

T(homas) S(tearns) Eliot was one of the outstanding writers of the 20th century. He wrote poems, plays, and essays, but he is probably best known for his poetry.

Born in St. Louis, Missouri, Eliot studied at Harvard, the Sorbonne in France, and Oxford in England. In 1914, he settled in London, where he worked as a bank clerk, teacher, editor, and publisher. Eliot became a British citizen in 1927.

His first important poem, "The Love Song of J. Alfred Prufrock," revealed his unique and complex poetic style, which Eliot developed with the help of Ezra Pound, an American poet. The poem shows the loneliness of an aging man, Prufrock, who fears the world. Eliot's long poetical work, "The Waste Land," contrasts the barrenness of modern society with societies of the past.

Eliot had very strong opinions about literature, modern life, and religion. He often wrote about the emptiness of modern life, but his later poems, such as "Ash Wednesday," express his feeling that Christianity gave meaning to life and offered hope to mankind. His later poems are very religious in feeling. But he also wrote in a lighter style. Eliot was extremely fond of cats and owned many of them. In 1939, he wrote a delightful book of nonsense poetry about cats, *Old Possum's Book of Practical Cats.* The famous musical "Cats" is based on this book.

T. S. Eliot was one of the most original poets of this century. His style has influenced many other modern poets. His plays stimulated more use of poetic drama in English. Two of Eliot's most famous plays are *Murder in the Cathedral* and *The Cocktail Party.* Like all his plays, they are written in unrhymed poetry and deal with religion and morality. Eliot's essays, giving his ideas about literature, have been a major influence on British and American critical writing. He was awarded the Nobel Prize for literature in 1948 and the U.S. Presidential Medal for freedom in 1964.

▶ ▶ ▶ ▶ **FIND OUT MORE** ◀ ◀ ◀ ◀
Literature; Nobel Prize; Poetry

ELIZABETH I (1533–1603)

Queen Elizabeth I of England was one of the world's greatest rulers. She became queen at the age of 25 and ruled for 45 years. The country prospered under her rule and became a great sea power. Great English writers who lived during Elizabeth's reign included William Shakespeare, Edmund Spenser, and the philosopher Francis Bacon.

Elizabeth was the daughter of Anne Boleyn, the second of the six wives of King Henry VIII. Her sickly half brother, Edward, was king for a short time. Then her half sister, Mary Tudor, was queen. When Mary died in 1558, Elizabeth became queen.

Elizabeth was tall, slim, and had red hair. She was a talented woman who loved fine clothes, jewels, music, and dancing. She picked wise advisers to help her run the country.

While Elizabeth was queen, Sir Francis Drake sailed around the world. His trips, and other trips by English sailors, opened up new markets for English goods. This period of peace and prosperity lasted for many years. But Spain wanted to control the seas. In 1588, Spain sent a huge fleet of more than one hundred ships—called the *Armada*—to attack England. Drake, aided by a storm, used smaller, faster ships to defeat the big Spanish ships.

Elizabeth never married. When she was dying, she agreed that James VI of Scotland should succeed her. He was the son of Elizabeth's cousin, Mary, Queen of Scots. The thrones of England and Scotland were united under James's rule.

▶ ▶ ▶ ▶ **FIND OUT MORE** ◀ ◀ ◀ ◀
Drake, Sir Francis; English History; Shakespeare, William; Spanish Armada

ELIZABETH II (1926–   )

Elizabeth II was crowned Queen of Great Britain in 1952. She is also head of the Commonwealth of Nations (an association of independent nations and dependent territories of the former British Empire). Her father was King George VI.

In 1947, Elizabeth married Philip Mountbatten, formerly Prince Philip of Greece. Philip was made Duke of Edinburgh shortly before their marriage.

Queen Elizabeth and her husband have four children: Prince Charles, Prince of Wales and heir to the throne, born in 1948; Princess Anne, born in 1950; Prince Andrew, born in 1960; and Prince Edward, born in 1964. The royal family name is Windsor, but Queen Elizabeth declared in 1960 that future descendants will be known as Mountbatten-Windsor.

Elizabeth is a constitutional monarch. Although head of state, she has no real political power. But she must read and sign all decrees passed by Parliament before they can

◀ **Elizabeth I, Queen of England. Her reign was an age of adventure and expanding power for England.**

Although Queen Elizabeth's birthday is on April 21, it is officially celebrated in June when the weather is better. She attends a colorful parade to review her troops.

▼ **Queen Elizabeth II on her coronation day in 1953. The two children in the foreground are Prince Charles and Princess Anne.**

EL SALVADOR

Capital city
San Salvador (973,000 people)

Area
8,124 square miles (21,041 sq. km)

Population
5,252,000 people

Government
Republic

Natural resources
Hydropower, crude oil, geothermal power

Export products
Coffee, cotton, sugar, shrimp

Unit of money
Colon

Official language
Spanish

become law. As a figurehead or symbol of the British government and people, she spends much of her time traveling abroad, paying official state visits to other countries, particularly Commonwealth nations. She also entertains foreign leaders when they come to Britain.

The queen enjoys country life, when she is not attending to official state business. She breeds dogs and horses, has a keen knowledge of horse racing, and is herself a good *equestrian* (rider).

▶▶▶▶ **FIND OUT MORE** ◀◀◀◀
Commonwealth of Nations; English History; George, Kings of Great Britain

EL SALVADOR

El Salvador is the smallest country in Central America, but it has more people per square mile than any Central American nation. This little country is tucked in along the Pacific Ocean between Guatemala and Honduras. It is the only Central American country without an Atlantic Ocean coast. Most Salvadorians are *mestizos*, people of mixed Spanish and Native Central American descent.

El Salvador is a country of clear lakes and beautiful beaches. It has a pleasant, mild climate except in the hot, humid, coastal lowlands. Two low volcanic mountain ranges cross the land—one near the coast and the other along the northern border. Between them is an upland of broad basins where most of El Salvador's people live. The large cities of San Salvador, the capital, and Santa Ana are located here, beside volcanoes.

Volcanic dust has settled on the valleys and slopes and made very fertile soil. Coffee bushes flourish on the cool hillsides and provide El Salvador's most valuable crop. A few very rich families own most of the coffee *fincas* (plantations).

Many Salvadorians make their living as farmers, raising cotton, beans, corn, rice, sugarcane, and *henequen*, a plant used for making rope and twine. Some Salvadorians work as farm laborers on coffee plantations. Families are large, and many children work in the fields with their parents. Some Salvadorians work in factories that produce textiles, leather goods, and chemicals. The government of El Salvador is keen to increase the number of industries in the nation, in an effort to reduce the country's dependence on single cash crops such as coffee.

Transportation of goods and passengers in El Salvador is sometimes difficult during the rainy season, when many roads cannot be used. But the big cities are connected by good bus lines, and the Inter-American Highway crosses the country from Guatemala to Honduras.

In 1524, Spaniards under Pedro de Alvarado conquered the Pipil and other native tribes in El Salvador. For almost 300 years, El Salvador was a Spanish colony. In 1821, it broke away from Spain and 20 years later

© 1994 GeoSystems, an R.R. Donnelley & Sons Company

became an independent republic. Political violence has often disrupted the country. El Salvador has waged war with Honduras over a border dispute, finally settled by treaty in 1980. Both rightist and leftist guerrilla groups have struggled for control of the government. During the 1980s, the United States supplied arms and training to the government army, which was engaged in a war with guerrilla rebels. José Napoleon Duarte was elected president in 1984. He died in 1990 and was succeeded by Alfredo Burkard.

▶▶▶▶ **FIND OUT MORE** ◀◀◀◀
Central America

ELVES AND FAIRIES

Tales of "little people," as elves and fairies are often called, are found in the folklore of many lands. According to these folklore tales, they are small, imaginary beings who sometimes help humans. Elves and fairies can disappear, fly, and change shape.

Elves are imaginary creatures of northern Europe. Good elves are said to be dainty and fair, and fond of music. Like so many of the little people, they love to dance. Other elves are bad. They live underground, away from sunlight. They are ugly, brown creatures. *Gnomes, dwarfs,* and *trolls* are usually bad elves.

In England, there is another kind of imaginary elf called a *pixie*. Pixies are attractive little sprites, always dressed in green. They do many things, mostly mischievous, such as leading travelers astray.

Fairies are charming little people in folktales. They also love to dance. Fairy rings, or circles of mushrooms, may be seen in forest clearings and in meadows. It was believed where the fairies have danced, no grass grows. It is not wise to disturb a fairy ring, because evil things may happen. If human beings should be so foolish as

to actually fall asleep in a fairy ring, they might be carried off to fairyland, or at the very least be severely pinched. Fairies can be quite helpful when they please. Sometimes, however, fairies are said to leave a *changeling* (an ugly, misshapen dwarf fairy) in the place of a human child.

Another kind of imaginary tiny spirits are the shaggy *brownies* of Scotland. In Germany they are called *kobolds.* Foot-high brownies are household creatures, who appreciate a neat, clean house. They will even help wash dishes and sweep floors. Brownies can create much mischief, however. They can make a cow's milk turn sour, or a horse go lame. To keep them happy, it is sensible to put out a bowl of cream and a bit of bread each night. Brownies are extremely fond of cream.

The Irish *leprechaun,* another imaginary creature, is supposed to look like a little old man. He stands about two feet tall and wears a tightly laced green coat, knee breeches, and buckled shoes. A leprechaun is highly skilled at making shoes. He is very, very rich and hides his money in a pot. If you should find a leprechaun, you might be able to persuade him to

▲ Because many European folktales are about elves and fairies, these traditional stories have become known as fairy tales. This fairy is from the tale, *The Three Wishes.*

▼ An elf dances for joy in the fairy tale *The Elves and the Shoemaker*. Elves love to dance, and are said to play music on golden harps.

WHERE TO DISCOVER MORE

Briggs, Katharine Mary.
An Encyclopedia of Fairies,
Hobgoblins, Brownies,
Bogies and Other
Supernatural Creatures.
New York: Pantheon
Books, 1977.

tell where his pot of gold is hidden. But he will just try to make you look away, and he will disappear!

Writers and musicians have enjoyed writing stories and composing music about elves and fairies. William Shakespeare wrote a play, *A Midsummer Night's Dream*. It is a story about a fairyland kingdom in which Oberon is the king, and Titania is the queen. Richard Wagner, a famous German composer, wrote a series of operas based on the *Nibelungs*, little creatures in Scandinavian and German mythology. The writer J.R.R. Tolkien included elves and dwarfs as characters in his three-volume story, *The Lord of the Rings*.

▶▶▶▶ **FIND OUT MORE** ◀◀◀◀
Fable; Fairy Tale; Grimm Brothers;
Opera; Shakespeare, William;
Wagner, Richard

EMANCIPATION PROCLAMATION

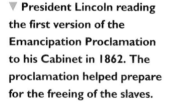

▼ **President Lincoln reading the first version of the Emancipation Proclamation to his Cabinet in 1862. The proclamation helped prepare for the freeing of the slaves.**

President Abraham Lincoln issued the Emancipation Proclamation during the Civil War. It was an important step in freeing the slaves. The proclamation was first announced publicly on September 22, 1862. Lincoln and his cabinet decided it would be a good time to issue the proclamation because the North had just won a victory over the South at the battle of Antietam. Lincoln's proclamation declared that, as of January 1, 1863, slaves "shall be then, thenceforward, and forever free." But the new law applied only to those slaves who were owned in those states that were fighting against the Union. It did not free the slaves in Maryland, Delaware, Kentucky, and Missouri—states that remained in the Union.

The Confederate States, of course, were not obeying the laws of the Union. So the proclamation had no effect on the slaves living in the South. The Emancipation Proclamation did not really free a single slave, but it paved the way for meaningful emancipation laws. The new state of West Virginia abolished slavery that same year, 1863. Maryland and Missouri voted to end slavery in 1864. In 1865, after the Civil War had ended, the Thirteenth Amendment to the Constitution was ratified, making slavery illegal in any part of the United States.

▶▶▶▶ **FIND OUT MORE** ◀◀◀◀
Abolition; Black Americans; Civil War;
Lincoln, Abraham; Slavery

EMBRYO

You have probably seen photographs taken of babies before they were born. Still inside his or her mother, the unborn child does not look quite like a fully formed baby. Yet it is growing and developing all the time. It is an *embryo*.

Whether it is human or animal, an embryo begins when a seed (*spermatozoon*) from the father meets an egg (*ovum*) from the mother and fertilizes it. Almost immediately the egg, which is a single cell, divides to form two cells. These in turn divide to make four cells, then eight, and so

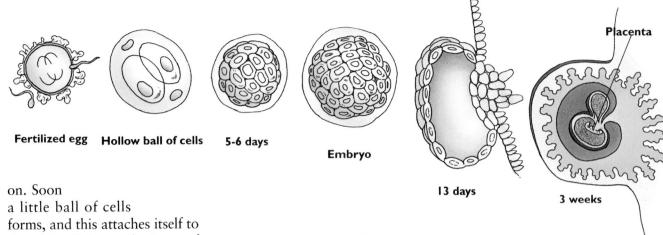

Fertilized egg **Hollow ball of cells** **5-6 days**

Embryo

13 days

Placenta

3 weeks

on. Soon
a little ball of cells
forms, and this attaches itself to
the walls of the mother's *womb*, or
uterus. Then the embryo divides into
four distinct layers. The outermost of
these is the *placenta*, which will help
the embryo to gain nourishment
from the mother. The other three
very swiftly start to develop into various
bodily organs, the heart being
one of the first to form.

After about eight weeks the human
embryo is usually called a *fetus*. During
this time it is looking more and
more like a newborn baby, and it is
growing bigger. By the time of its
birth, the fetus will have developed
fingers and toes, eyes, nose, ears, hair,
and sometimes teeth. It is ready to be
born as a new individual.

▶▶▶▶ **FIND OUT MORE** ◀◀◀◀
Egg; Reproduction

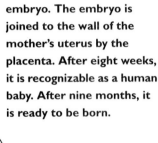

4 weeks

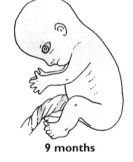

8 weeks

9 months

◀ **A baby begins life as
a fertilized egg, which
develops quickly into an
embryo. The embryo is
joined to the wall of the
mother's uterus by the
placenta. After eight weeks,
it is recognizable as a human
baby. After nine months, it
is ready to be born.**

EMERSON, RALPH WALDO
(1803–1882)

The philosophy of Ralph Waldo
Emerson expressed many of the
finest ideas of early America. He
taught that "God is in every man"
and in all natural things. He believed
that every person should follow his
own conscience, even if his ideas did
not agree with those of other people
or the rules of society. A person could
find inner peace and live an honest
life only by complete self-reliance.
Emerson thought that a person could
best experience the presence of God
within himself when he was alone
and close to nature. He also felt God

revealed him-
self in nature and
that people could
understand God
better by getting
closer to nature.

Emerson was
brought up in
Boston, Massachu-
setts. He became a
minister of the Unitarian Church. But
he found that he could not both follow
his own philosophy and obey the
rules of the church. He left the
church and later settled in Concord,
Massachusetts. He wrote down the
basic ideas of his philosophy in 1836
in his first book, *Nature*. He also
wrote poems and essays and gave lectures.
Emerson's ideas inspired many
people of his own day. His belief in
the individual freedom of all people
greatly influenced later American
thinkers and writers, including Herman
Melville and Walt Whitman.

▶▶▶▶ **FIND OUT MORE** ◀◀◀◀
Literature

▼ **Ralph Waldo Emerson,
American philosopher.**

Although scientists for years have been trying to find out exactly how our emotions work, they have not yet found the answer. This applies especially to the relationship between our emotions and our body reactions. Most people agree, however, that many disorders can be caused by emotional strain. These include asthma, hay fever, migraine headaches, some heart complaints, and the putting on or losing of too much weight.

▼ Our faces show how we feel. This girl is frightened of a spider. Her face shows that the emotion she feels is fear.

 ## EMOTION

Have you ever been angry at someone, or afraid of something? Do you love someone special? Do you know that some people hate other people?. Anger and fear, love and hate are *emotions*. Some other emotions are joy, hope, delight, despair, sadness, and disgust. Everyone has emotions.

Emotions come upon you suddenly. You do not *think* emotions, you *feel* them. You do not think, "This is an uncaged tiger. I have heard that tigers sometimes kill and eat human beings. I am a human being, so I will now be afraid of the tiger." Instead, you feel afraid instantly upon finding yourself near a tiger out of its cage.

Emotions can be aroused when information comes to you through your senses. You *see* someone dear to you, and you feel love. You *hear* a scraping sound in a dark room, and you feel fear. You *smell* an unpleasant odor, and you feel disgusted. Emotions can also be aroused by thoughts. You think of someone who

hurt you, and you feel anger or hate. You think of a test you are not ready to take, and you feel fear or sense defeat.

Thoughts you are not aware of can also bring out emotions. These are called *unconscious* thoughts. For instance, when you were very small, you may have been scared by a big, barking dog. You forgot about this unpleasant happening, but it is stored in your unconscious memory. You may now be nervous around big dogs.

People seem to be born with a few emotions and gradually learn the rest. A newborn baby fears falling and loud sounds, yet it does not seem to fear anything else. Babies must learn to be afraid of fire, dangerous animals, and other things that can harm them. The fears of falling and loud sounds do not have to be learned.

The word "emotion" comes from the Latin word *exmovere*, meaning "to move away, or to stir up." Your emotions move you, carry you away, stir you up, cause you to act. Joy may make you jump up and down, clap your hands, and smile or laugh. Fear may make you run and scream, or stand and tremble.

Emotions also affect your body in ways of which you are not aware. Fear causes the adrenal glands to secrete into your blood a chemical substance called *adrenalin*. Adrenalin makes your heart beat faster, your blood pressure rise, and your breathing become faster. It also causes blood to go from your stomach and intestines to your muscles, stopping digestion. Sugar stored in your muscles and liver is sent into your blood. You may tremble and perspire. Your body is ready to react to what is causing your fear. You may run away, or try to fight or hide.

▶ ▶ ▶ ▶ **FIND OUT MORE** ◀ ◀ ◀ ◀
Freud, Sigmund; Mental Health; Psychology

EMPIRE STATE BUILDING

The Empire State Building, located on Fifth Avenue in New York City, is one of the tallest buildings in the world. Only the Sears Tower in Chicago and the World Trade Center (Twin Towers) in New York City are taller.

The Empire State Building, built between 1930 and 1931, cost almost $41 million. It has a steel structure and its 102 stories reach 1,250 feet (381 m) high. A television broadcasting tower, with a beacon on top, brings the total height to 1,454 feet (443 m). For 42 years, the Empire State Building was the tallest building in the world.

This famous skyscraper houses about 10,000 office people. Every year more than 1½ million tourists ride the high-speed elevators to the observation decks. During storms, the building may sway an inch or more from center, as most skyscrapers do.

▶▶▶▶ **FIND OUT MORE** ◀◀◀◀
Architecture; Construction

ENAMELING

Enameling is an art form in which colored glass is *fused* (united by melting together) to a metal base. The combination of fused glass and metal is called enamel. The glass used in enameling is not the ordinary kind that cracks as it cools. Enameling glass is a colorless powder, with

metallic oxides added for color. Hobbyists today can buy enamel in powdered form in a wide variety of bright colors.

Enameling is a very ancient craft. Both Chinese and Egyptian art pieces and jewelry can be seen in museums. The Byzantines (peoples of ancient Istanbul) did beautiful enameling during the tenth and eleventh centuries. Thin strips of metal were applied to metal objects. The compartments created by the strips were filled with enamel. This process is called *cloisonné*. St. Mark's Cathedral, in Venice, Italy, has 81 enameled plaques in the altarpiece. Benvenuto Cellini's famous enameled chalice is on display at the Metropolitan Museum of Art in New York City.

Hobbyists and artists can make many kinds of enameled objects, such as cuff links, ashtrays, bracelets, rings, pins, and plaques. Copper is the most popular metal for this craft.

Enameling is an "art of fire," so a *kiln*, or very hot oven, is needed. Art supply stores sell

▲ This enameled vase was created in China during the early 1400s. A decorative enameling technique called *cloisonné* was used to fuse the colors to the vase.

▲ Although this box from the Ming Dynasty in China is about 500 years old, its enameled surface has kept the patterns and colors strong and bright.

▶ New York City's Empire State Building has 102 stories and stands 1,250 feet (381 m) tall. Its foundations extend 56 feet (17m) into the ground.

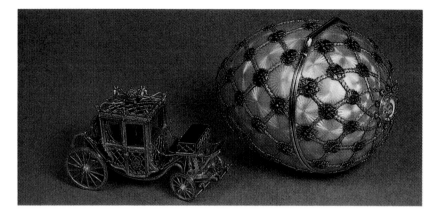

▲ This miniature carriage and egg are examples of fine enameling, a decorative art practiced since ancient times.

Chinese scholars produced the largest encyclopedia ever written. In the 1600s, more than 2,000 writers worked to put together the *Yung Lo Ta Tien* encyclopedia for their emperor. This encyclopedia was bound into 11,100 volumes.

▲ An illustrated page from *Natural History*, an encyclopedia written by the Roman Pliny the Elder.

910

inexpensive kilns, which are small electric coil heaters.

▶▶▶▶ **FIND OUT MORE** ◀◀◀◀
Pottery and China

ENCYCLOPEDIA

The word "encyclopedia" comes from two Greek words meaning "a circle of learning." A general encyclopedia is a book or a series of books containing the important facts about the most significant people, places, objects, events, and ideas known to mankind. Other encyclopedias offer more detailed information about special subjects, such as science or music. Some encyclopedias are written especially for children. The information in most encyclopedias is written in the form of articles, which are usually arranged alphabetically.

The oldest encyclopedia that is still in existence was written in the first century A.D. by a Roman scholar named Pliny the Elder. His encyclopedia, called *Natural History,* has 37 volumes. It covers many subjects, including biology, medicine, art, geography, and agriculture. Pliny spent many years reading books and writing short articles on what he thought was important in each subject. Denis Diderot and Jean d'Alembert, two French

writers, edited a 28-volume encyclopedia (*encyclopedie* in French) between 1751 and 1772. It contained articles on history and science as well as criticism of the way people lived.

Until the 1800s, encyclopedias were written mainly as reference works for scholars. But most modern encyclopedias are designed to offer interesting and useful information to the general reader. Encyclopedias today are written by expert authors, whose articles are put together by editors to make attractive books. Most encyclopedias are illustrated with photographs, maps, diagrams, and art works. Encyclopedias are sometimes kept up-to-date by the addition of a new book each year. This new book, called a "yearbook," has articles about important events from the year before. Some encyclopedias are reprinted often to include new information. One of the oldest and most important encyclopedias of this type is the *Encyclopaedia Britannica,* first published in Edinburgh, Scotland, between 1768 and 1771.

The Young Students Learning Library is an encyclopedia that is intended to inform young people

▲ Denis Diderot's 28-volume *Encyclopedie* was published between 1751 and 1772.

about the world in which they live, and to help them understand ideas and language. It has been written to help children in school.

The Young Students Learning Library has more than 3,500 articles arranged in alphabetical order and 5,000 photos and illustrations. It has an index in volume 23 that provides more than 20,000 entries. The Young Students Learning Library also comes with an atlas and a dictionary. Cross-references, such as FIND OUT MORE, are included at the end of most articles. These tell you which other articles in this encyclopedia offer further information on a particular subject.

The "Learn by Doing" activities in many of the articles are the most unique feature of this encyclopedia. They contain suggestions for ways to use the knowledge in the articles. These suggestions are fun to follow, because by doing so you find out about things for yourself.

One of the first American encyclopedias for children was the *Book of Knowledge*. It was first published in 1910. The articles in this encyclopedia were not in an alphabetical order. Instead the encyclopedia was organized *thematically*. The information was contained in articles on major topics. For instance, a topic such as "animal life" covered a great many animals in one article. The encyclopedia also had many stories, poems, and games.

▶▶▶▶ **FIND OUT MORE** ◀◀◀◀
Reference Book

⚙ ENERGY

"I'm so tired. I don't have the energy to do anything!" What do people mean when they say this? Scientists say that energy is the capacity to do work. So energy is needed to make any kind of action happen. A person must *expend* (use) energy to throw a

---

LEARN BY DOING

Think how you would plan your own miniature encyclopedia. What title would you pick for your encyclopedia? How would you arrange your subjects—in alphabetical order, as in the *Young Students Learning Library*? Perhaps you would want to have an encyclopedia just on animals or sports, or some other special subject you especially like. Would you have separate volumes? How many?

Look up the information on your subjects in the *Young Students Learning Library*. Try to write in your own words, instead of copying directly from the encyclopedia. Where would you get the pictures you need for your articles? From magazines and newspapers? Photographs that your family has taken? You might like to draw or paint your own pictures. When you finish your encyclopedia, you will want to keep it in order by stapling or clipping it together, or binding it in folders or notebooks.

---

ball, ride a bicycle, or climb a tree. All of these activities are work.

Energy must be used to do work. The amount of work done is the same as the energy necessary to do it. Both are measured by the distance an object moves and the force needed to move the object. The scientific unit of energy and work is the *joule*, which is the energy needed or work done when a force of 1 *newton* moves an object 1 meter. The joule is not a large unit; you need about 1,000 joules of energy to climb a flight of stairs, for example. Another unit of energy is the *foot-pound*.

Kinds of Energy

Work is done in several ways. Each way needs a different type of energy.

POTENTIAL ENERGY. If you have a model airplane driven by a rubber band, you give it power by turning the propeller, which winds (stretches) the rubber band. As long as you hold the propeller, nothing can happen. But the rubber band has a *potential* ability to do work. That is, the rubber band may do work in the future. The stretched rubber band has *potential energy*, or energy of position. So does a hammer held high above a nail, or water held by a dam at the top of a hill.

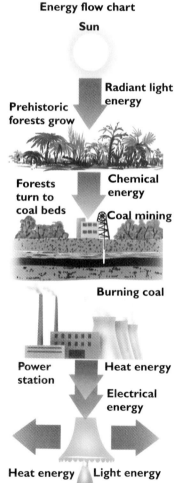

Energy flow chart

Sun

Radiant light energy

Prehistoric forests grow

Chemical energy

Forests turn to coal beds

Coal mining

Burning coal

Power station

Heat energy

Electrical energy

Heat energy   **Light energy**

▲ The sun is the source of most of the energy that we use for living. Every time it is used, energy is converted from one form to another.

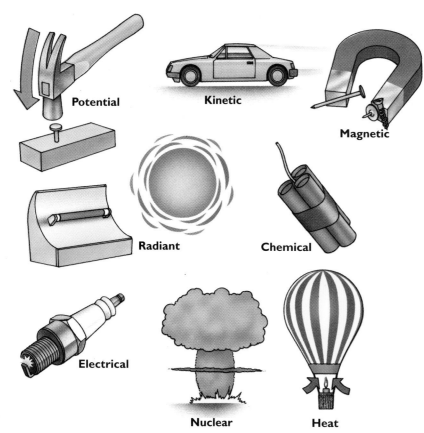

Potential

Kinetic

Magnetic

Radiant

Chemical

Electrical

Nuclear

Heat

▲ Energy is needed to make any action happen. Here are examples of the different forms of energy.

▼ Generators built across a river convert tidal power into electricity. The rising tide flows through turbines; when the tide falls, water runs through the turbines in the opposite directions

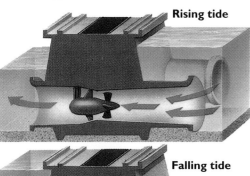

Rising tide

Falling tide

KINETIC ENERGY. Let go of the propeller of your airplane. The rubber band now has kinetic energy, or energy of motion. It is doing actual work. So is a hammer falling on a nail, or water running downhill and turning a waterwheel. Potential and kinetic energy together are sometimes called *mechanical energy.*

ELECTRICAL ENERGY. Electricity has *electrical energy.* It produces force in electric machines, such as an electric motor, so that they can do work. Electricity can also produce heat and light, which are other forms of energy that do work.

SOUND AND LIGHT ENERGY. Sound can do work, and so can light. These are two very different forms of energy. Light is a part of a very large group of radiations, including X rays, ultraviolet rays, infrared rays, microwaves, and radio waves. All of these electromagnetic radiations behave much like light, and together

they are all forms of *radiant energy.* The sun is an intense source of radiant energy.

CHEMICAL ENERGY. The atoms of any chemical compound are normally held together by powerful forces. Chemical compounds have potential energy, just like a hammer held in the air. If the atoms are freed from their positions—if their bonds are broken—they move and may release heat, or other forms of energy. You can see that *chemical energy* can be very powerful if you think of a stick of dynamite or a tank of gasoline.

NUCLEAR ENERGY. The nuclei of atoms are made up of tiny particles. The forces that hold these particles together are far stronger than the forces that hold whole atoms in place. When these forces are overcome, a release of energy much more violent than that produced by dynamite occurs. Nuclear explosions are examples of *nuclear energy.*

HEAT ENERGY. If you were the pilot of a hot-air balloon, you would turn on the gas burner to make your balloon rise higher and turn off the burner to descend. You would be using *heat energy* to fly.

Changing and Measuring Energy

One form of energy can be changed into another form. Chemical energy is changed into light energy and heat energy when wood is burned. In an electric light bulb, or in a toaster, electric energy is changed into light energy and heat energy. In an electric motor, electric energy is turned into kinetic energy.

The joule can be used to measure energy and work in all its forms. An electric current of 1 ampere flowing through a resistance of 1 ohm for 1 second does 1 joule of work. Heating 1 gram (0.035 oz.) of water by 0.24°C (32.43°F) requires 1 joule of heat energy. The energy value of food is frequently measured in larger energy units called calories. One calorie equals 4,186 joules. You need about 2,000 calories from food and drink every day. The chemical energy in the food and drink changes to heat energy to keep you warm, and to kinetic energy in your muscles.

The Conservation of Energy

Energy sometimes seems to vanish. A bouncing ball makes smaller and smaller bounces and finally comes to rest. Has its energy disappeared? No. The energy has changed, however, from kinetic energy to sound energy, as the ball strikes the ground, and also to heat. Some of the energy heated the air that the moving ball pushed through. The rest of the energy heated the ground that the ball touched or the ball itself.

If you examine every use of energy, you will discover that energy never vanishes. It may change several times, and it always ends up as heat or radiant energy, which escapes from the Earth.

All energy has a source. To give electrical energy to a flashlight bulb, a battery must use its chemical energy. The bulb then expends the electrical energy to produce light energy.

These facts make up a basic rule, or law, of physics—the law of conservation of energy: *Energy may be changed from one form to another, but it can never be created or destroyed.* This is called the first law of *thermodynamics* (the study of all forms of energy).

This law is true most of the time. But scientists have discovered special situations in which energy can vanish. When this happens, new matter appears to "replace" the energy. Matter can also vanish, to be replaced by energy. A new law of physics—*the law of conservation of mass and energy*—has been worked out. This law says that the total amount of mass and energy is constant. If one is destroyed, an equivalent amount of the other is created.

Energy is necessary to life. The

▲ **The sun is an immense source of energy. This solar furnace in France uses that energy by focusing the sun's rays by means of a huge curved mirror. This furnace can produce temperatures of around 5400°F (3,000°C).**

basic energy of life comes from the heat of the sun. Green plants use this energy. Animals get their energy from eating green plants or from eating other animals that have eaten the plants. Much modern industry depends on potential energy stored millions of years ago in fossil fuels—coal, oil, and gas. We are rapidly using up these energy sources and need new ones. Satellites in orbit and space probes far distant from the Earth may get their energy from solar cells, which convert sunlight into electricity. Energy produced by bombarding certain atoms with certain particles has given us nuclear energy. Scientists are working to increase the energy available, obtained by harnessing the power of winds and tides.

▶▶▶▶ **FIND OUT MORE** ◀◀◀◀
History see Einstein, Albert; Galileo; Newton, Sir Isaac
Kinds of Energy see Electric Power; Heat and Cold; Nuclear Energy
Sources and Effects of Energy see Atom; Battery; Coal; Electricity; Engine; Explosives; Friction; Fuel; Fuel Cell; Gravity and Gravitation; Light; Magnet; Motion; Motor; Petroleum; Sound; Sun

The United States uses more energy per person than any other country. The average U.S. citizen uses the equivalent of about 30,000 pounds or 13,600 kg of coal a year. This means that we each need the energy from 15 tons of coal every year. In poor countries such as Burundi and Rwanda (in Africa) the average energy consumption per person is only about 200 pounds of coal.

▲ The Greek inventor Hero built the first steam engine. Steam escaped from two spouts pointing in opposite directions, making the metal ball spin on its axis.

▶ Thomas Newcomen's engine was used to pump water out of mines. Steam from a boiler pushed up a piston. A jet of cold water caused the piston to fall again.

⚙ ENGINE

Engines are devices that change stored (potential) energy into useful mechanical energy. People have used some kind of engine—especially windmills and waterwheels—for many hundreds of years. But when the air is calm, windmills are useless. When rivers and lakes run dry, waterwheels will stop. Other kinds of engines have been developed, because they are more reliable than nature and also stronger than people and the draft animals, such as horses, we have trained to work for us.

Steam Engines

Steam engines are really very old. The first one known was invented by Hero, a Greek who lived in Egypt nearly 2,000 years ago. His engine did no work, but it must have been wonderful to watch, because no one—including Hero—understood how it worked. In fact, no one knew for more than 1,500 years how Hero's engine worked.

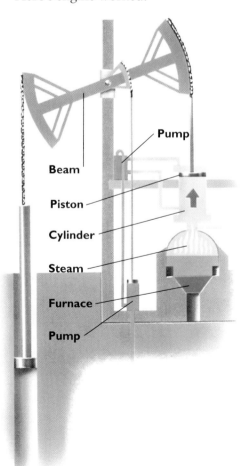

Beam

Pump

Piston

Cylinder

Steam

Furnace

Pump

In 1687, Isaac Newton gave an explanation of how the engine worked. Newton developed three laws (rules) of motion. The third law says, "For every action there is an equal but opposite reaction." This law sounds complicated, but it is really very simple. You "use" *action-reaction* every time you walk. You push one way on the ground (action), and the ground pushes *you* in the opposite direction (reaction). You move, instead of the ground, because you weigh much less than the Earth. (The Earth really *does* move when you push against it, but it weighs so much its movement is too small to be measured.)

You have seen action-reaction many times. When you jump off a skateboard (action), the empty skateboard rolls forward (reaction). If you blow up a balloon and let it go, the air shoots out the open end (action), and the balloon shoots around the room until nearly all the air inside the balloon is used up (reaction).

Hero's engine worked much like the balloon. It was a kind of reaction *turbine*. A *turbine* is an engine that produces power by rotating. Giovanni Branca, an Italian, invented another kind of turbine in 1629. In this, a jet of steam from an outside source turned a wheel by striking the blades into which the wheel was divided. This engine was a kind of *impulse turbine*.

The first steam engines to do real work were *reciprocating engines*. Thomas Newcomen's *atmospheric engine* of the early 1700s used air pressure to do the work. Like true steam engines, it had a *piston* (plunger) inside a *cylinder* (tube). One end of the piston was connected to a pump handle in such a way that the weight of the handle pulled the piston to the top of the cylinder. Steam flowed into the cylinder below the rising piston. When the piston reached the top of the cylinder, the steam was shut off, and cold water was shot into the cylinder. The water caused the steam to *condense* (turn back into water). This caused a vacuum below the piston. The air pressure above the piston forced the piston down the cylinder, raising the pump handle. Then the cycle started all over again.

Newcomen's engine was slow and used large quantities of steam. James Watt improved the piston engine by designing one in which steam flowed first into one end of the cylinder and then into the other end, moving the piston first one way, then the other. This was a true steam engine, since steam did all the work. A *condenser* turned the used steam into hot water and fed it back to the boiler. This helped save fuel, since the water entered the boiler hot, and also created a vacuum that helped draw steam through the engine.

Every kind of steam engine depends upon one fact: when a quantity of water is heated and turned into steam, the steam takes up 1,700 times as much room as the water did. If water turns into steam in a closed container (such as a boiler), the water cannot expand, so it produces pressure, or force. In all steam engines, the water is heated in a boiler and then piped to the engine. The fuel is burned outside the engine. For this reason, steam engines are called *external combustion* engines.

Modern steam engines are almost always turbines. A turbine weighs less and runs more smoothly than a piston engine that can do the same amount of work. Steam turbines are often used to power ships and to generate electricity. They are harder to maintain than a piston engine, however.

Internal Combustion Engines

In an *internal combustion* engine, fuel is burned inside the engine itself. The most common kind of internal combustion engine is the *gasoline piston* engine, which is used to power automobiles. Most automobile

▲ In 1775, the Scottish inventor James Watt patented his design for a steam engine. He built engines that forced the steam to act on both sides of the piston, and also invented an outside *condenser* to turn waste steam back into water.

▼ George Stephenson completed the *Rocket* steam locomotive in 1829. It could produce steam more quickly and with less fuel than earlier locomotives. On its trial run the *Rocket* reached a speed of 29½ miles per hour (47 km/hr).

▲ George Stephenson, British engineer who built the first steam locomotive.

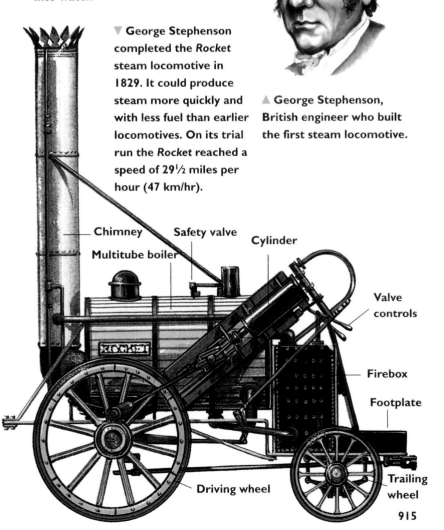

Chimney

Safety valve

Cylinder

Multitube boiler

Valve controls

Firebox

Footplate

Driving wheel

Trailing wheel

▶ In a four-stroke automobile engine, the induction stroke pulls a fuel and air mixture into the cylinder. The second stroke compresses the mixture, and the third stroke ignites it to produce power to turn the wheels. The fourth stroke forces exhaust gases out of the cylinder.

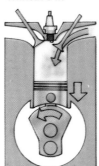
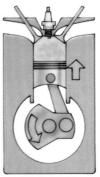
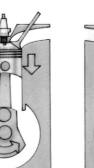
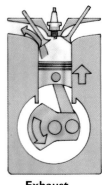

Fuel and air mixture in

Air and fuel mixture compressed

Combustion

Exhaust gases escape

Induction **Compression** **Power** **Exhaust**

▲ In 1885, the German engineer Gottlieb Daimler built an internal combustion engine that ran on gasoline. He used the engine to turn the wheels of a bicycle.

▼ The Wankel or rotary engine is unusual, because it has a rotating piston that sucks in fuel and air. This mixture is compressed and ignited by a spark to produce power.

engines consist of several cylinders arranged in one or two rows. Inside each cylinder is a piston and a *spark plug,* a device that produces sparks. A mixture of air and gasoline is forced into the cylinder and compressed. Then a spark from the spark plug causes an explosion giving the piston a mighty push down the cylinder. The pistons of an automobile engine are connected to a rod, called a crankshaft. As a piston moves down the cylinder, it causes the crankshaft to turn. When the engine is adjusted so that the cylinders "fire" one after another, the crankshaft is kept turning constantly. The crankshaft is connected to the wheels by a complicated series of gears, so that as it turns, it turns the wheels.

Gasoline engines unfortunately pollute the air with their exhaust gases. New automobiles are fitted with *catalytic converters,* which remove poisonous substances from

the exhaust gases. Many cars of the future will be powered by electricity, solar power, and other energy that does not pollute the air.

Small airplanes are usually powered by gasoline piston engines. The crankshaft is connected to the propeller, not the wheels. And the cylinders are most often arranged in a circle, not in straight lines. This is called a radial engine design.

One other kind of piston engine is the *diesel* engine. It has no spark plugs. Instead, it depends upon very hot air to cause the explosions that provide the power.

GAS TURBINE. A gas turbine is very much like a steam turbine. But a gas other than steam does the work of turning the engine wheels, and the fuel is burned inside the engine, not outside.

JET AND ROCKET ENGINES. These are action-reaction engines. Hero's steam engine, which de-

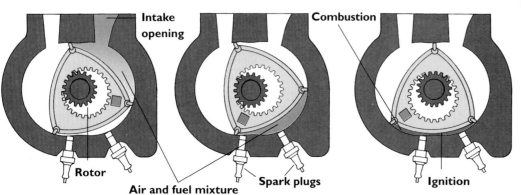
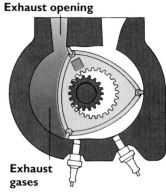

Intake opening

Combustion

Exhaust opening

Rotor

Air and fuel mixture

Spark plugs

Ignition

Exhaust gases

Intake **Compression** **Power** **Exhaust**

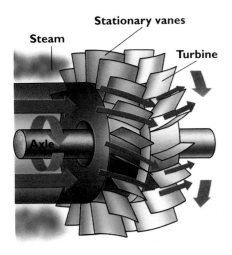

Steam Stationary vanes Turbine Axle

▲ A turbine increases in power when steam is directed with stationary vanes before it reaches the turbine blades.

LEARN BY DOING

In gasoline and diesel engines, up-down motion has to be changed into rotary motion to turn wheels. This is done by the piston and crankshaft. You can see how they work if you make an L-shaped cardboard bracket. Push a pencil through the upright end and slide a cotton reel over the pencil. Pin a straw to the cotton reel. Move the straw (or piston) up and down to make it drive the cotton reel (crankshaft) round.

pended on external combustion, was actually a reaction turbine, not a jet engine as we know it. Modern jet and rocket engines are internal combustion engines. In both jet and rocket engines, hot gases shoot out of the rear of the engine (action), pushing the engine—and the airplane or rocket attached to the engine—forward (reaction). The major difference between these two engines is that jets need oxygen from the atmosphere to burn with the fuel, while rocket engines carry oxygen with them so that they can work outside the atmosphere, in space.

▶▶▶▶ **FIND OUT MORE** ◀◀◀◀
Automobile; Diesel Engine; Fuel; Gasoline; Jet Propulsion; Motor; Rocket; Vacuum; Watt, James

⚙ ENGINEERING

Have you ever thought about inventing something new and useful? You may have had a good idea, but you lacked the knowledge to design, build, and make your invention. Engineering involves all of these steps. Engineers must know how to plan and design structures, machinery, appliances, and many other things. Engineers must know what materials to use and how to put those materials together. They must also know how to produce the things they design efficiently.

Engineers are sometimes clever detectives. Here is an example of engineering detective work. A museum owned a painting that was said to have been made in the 1400s. An art expert thought it was a forgery. The museum did not want to scrape paint from the picture for analysis. A sample had to be obtained without harming the painting.

The diesel engine is more efficient than the gasoline engine. More useful work is done for each gallon of fuel used. But diesel engines have their disadvantages, too. They have to be heavier than gasoline engines and are more expensive.

A jet engine weighs less than a piston engine of the same power and can be much more streamlined.

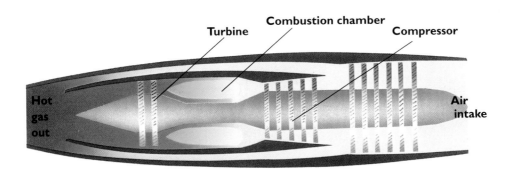

Turbine Combustion chamber Compressor Air intake Hot gas out

◀ In a turbofan engine, a mixture of air and burning fuel expands and forces its way out of the exhaust. This backward blast of hot gas pushes an airplane forward.

▲ **Engineers work on a city drainage system during the 1800s, a time of rapid growth of industrial cities.**

▼ **The Channel Tunnel runs beneath the English Channel linking France to England. A giant cutting device called a tunnel boring machine (TBM) was used to dig the tunnel.**

Two engineers invented a research tool called a *microprobe*. The microprobe is a hollow needle with a diameter 25 times smaller than that of a human hair! The needle was pushed into the painting, making an invisible hole. Then it was pulled out, carrying a core of the paint. Analysis showed that the paint contained titanium oxide. Titanium oxide was not in use before 1920, so the painting could not have been made in the 1400s. It was a forgery.

The inventors of the microprobe were *metallurgical* engineers. Metallurgical engineers work in two areas. One area involves ways to get metal from raw ore and to refine the metal. The other area concerns metals after they are refined, and ways to combine them into alloys. *Metallurgy* is only one of a number of engineering fields open to young people.

The oldest engineering profession is that of civil engineer. Civil engineers build bridges, tunnels, roads, and buildings. You see examples of their work every day. A special branch of civil engineering is *hydraulic* engineering, which deals with such projects as widening rivers

▲ **A worker helping to construct San Francisco's Golden Gate Bridge, one of the great engineering achievements of the early 1900s.**

or building canals or dams. *Hydroelectric* engineering uses water for generating electricity.

Another civil engineering branch is *sanitary* engineering. Among other things, sanitary engineering is concerned with water and air pollution, food sanitation, sewage treatment and disposal, and pest control. Many more sanitary engineers are needed

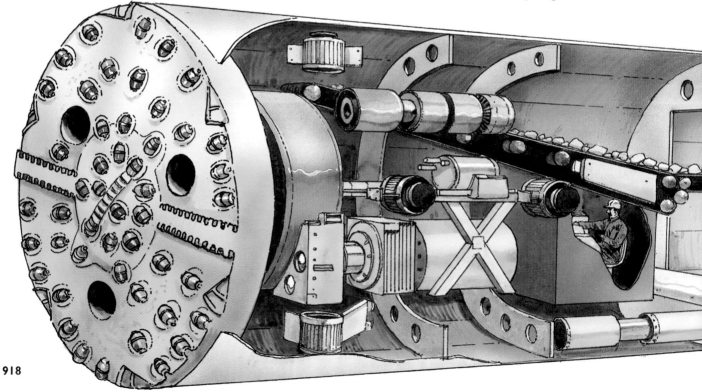

to deal with these service problems in today's world.

There are many other engineering specialties. *Mechanical* engineering, for instance, is primarily concerned with machines. But mechanical engineering also includes branches dealing with automobiles, aeronautics, refrigeration, and ventilation, among other fields.

Mechanical engineers may work closely with *chemical* engineers. A chemical engineer develops new chemicals and designs and builds machines that manufacture numerous products, such as toothpaste, medicines, perfumes, plastics, and cloth.

Another interesting field is that of the *agricultural* engineer. These experts apply general engineering knowledge to large-scale farming operations. For instance, they may be concerned with farm buildings, water supplies, milk coolers, farm machinery, electricity, or heating and ventilation, among other possibilities.

Mining engineers often work deep within the Earth. They make surveys, operate drills, and work on various kinds of machines. Mining engineers need knowledge of mechanical, civil, electrical, metallurgical, and even some chemical engineering to carry out their work effectively.

In our "computer age," an important field is that of *electrical* and *electronics* engineering. An electrical engineer deals mostly with problems involving wiring and the transmission of electricity over wires. An electronics engineer may be concerned with wireless transmissions, such as radio, radar, and television. Electronics engineers are also working in advanced areas of computing, communications, navigation, and robotics—making new kinds of machines that can almost think for themselves. *Nuclear* engineers deal with ways to use and control the power contained inside atoms. They often work closely with electronics engineers.

Oceanographic engineering deals with studies of the oceans and ocean floors. This specialty requires a knowledge of civil, mechanical, geological, electrical, mining, and other engineering fields.

The new field of *cryogenic* engineering involves working with materials, processes, and equipment used at temperatures as low as -456°F (-271°C). This intense cold is attained by the use of liquid oxygen, nitrogen, and other gases, all of which are so cold that ordinary ice is hot by comparison. Cryogenic engineering is important in space exploration and food processing.

One of the world's greatest engineering achievements was the building of the Canadian National Tower in Toronto. It is the highest tower in the world that is not supported by cables. To build it, a huge hole was dug and thousands of tons of concrete were poured into it to form the biggest raft foundation in the world. Specially built cranes lifted the building materials as high as 1,500 feet (460 m). Above that height, a big helicopter was used to lift the tower pieces, bit by bit. The television mast on the top of the tower is 1,814 feet (553 m) high.

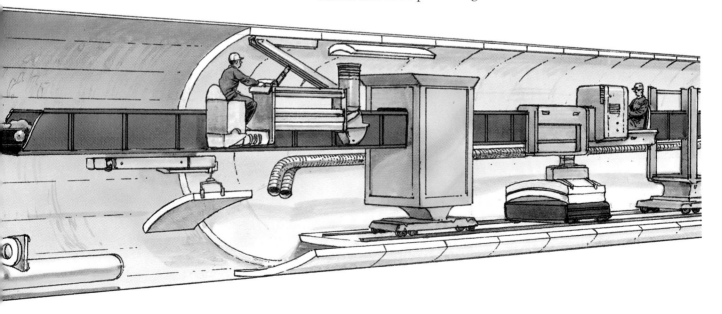

 A view of Kimmeridge Bay, on the Isle of Purbeck, England. This view is typical of the idyllic pastoral Dorset landscape.

Another new field of engineering is *genetic* engineering. This deals with the creation of new biological organisms, and with the techniques of handling genes (the "building blocks" of living things) to improve our treatment of disease, and develop improved breeds of plants.

If you enjoy taking things apart to find out how they work, and if you enjoy science and mathematics in school, you may someday want to be an engineer.

▶ ▶ ▶ ▶ **FIND OUT MORE** ◀ ◀ ◀ ◀

Agriculture; Computer; Construction; Cryogenics; Electronics; Genetics; Hydraulics; Machine; Metallurgy; Mines and mining; Nuclear energy; Robot; Sanitation

ENGLAND

"This royal throne of kings, this sceptered isle....This precious stone set in the silver sea....This blessed plot, this earth, this realm, this England." So did the playwright William Shakespeare describe England in his play *King Richard II*.

England is the largest of the four once-separate countries that make up the United Kingdom of Great Britain and Northern Ireland. Besides Northern Ireland, the other countries of the United Kingdom are Scotland and Wales. (See the map with the article on the BRITISH ISLES.)

London is the capital city of the United Kingdom and its largest city. England is bordered by ocean (the North Sea and the English Channel) on the east and south, and borders on Scotland to the north and Wales to the west. In the far west of England lies a *peninsula* (strip of land) washed by the Atlantic Ocean. The highest land is in the west. The mountains called the Pennine Chain begin at the border of Scotland and run through central England. In the middle of the country are the rolling hills and valleys called the Midlands. The land is flat and low in the east, in the region known as East Anglia.

Although England is farther north than the northeastern United States, its climate is mild and rainy. In winter, temperatures usually stay above 20°F (6°C) and in summer below 80°F (27°C). A warm ocean current called the Gulf Stream flows up from the equator, then turns east to meet the Continental Drift in the Atlantic, which flows north and passes the coast of England. Winds blowing

▼ Although England has many built-up areas, people can quickly get away to the peace of the countryside. A church, with its churchyard full of old headstones, is a good place to start exploring. This is Holy Trinity church at Long Melford, Suffolk, in eastern England.

across this current bring warm air to England in the winter.

England's natural resources include coal, iron ore, petroleum, and natural gas from the North Sea. It is an industrial trading country, preparing goods for sale in other countries, and handling international banking and insurance. England became successful as a trading country because it had a good transportation system, an excellent merchant marine, good seaports, and is close to the European mainland. England is the leading industrial country of the United Kingdom, with southeast England being the nation's richest and most populous area.

The Industrial Revolution began in English textile factories in the 1700s. Today, aerospace equipment, cars, electronic goods, and textiles are among the goods manufactured.

Although about four-fifths of England's land is used for farming, England still must import about half of its food. English farms are generally smaller than American farms. A large part of the land is used for the grazing of beef and dairy cattle and sheep. The main crops are grains, potatoes, vegetables, and fruits.

The names "England" and "English" come from an early tribe, the Angles, who conquered part of the Saxon land in the late fifth century A.D. The English language comes from many sources. These include Latin (brought by the Romans and Anglo-Saxons) and Norman French (brought in 1066 by the followers of William the Conqueror from Normandy). Many English words are spelled differently from the way they are in the United States. The word "color," for example, is spelled "colour" in England.

Soccer is the most popular sport in England. People call it "football" but it is not like American football. Up to 100,000 people may turn out for soccer matches. Cricket and rugby are also popular in England.

▲ **Bridges old and new stretch across the Mersey river in the heavily industrialized Merseyside region in north-west England. Liverpool is Merseyside's principal city.**

Traditions are a very important part of English public life. Perhaps because of these strong traditions some English people resist the idea of union with the rest of Europe. The royal family still holds an important place in the nation's life, although the monarch no longer has any real power of government. England has much to interest visitors—historic castles and houses, varied scenery, quiet country villages, and a rich culture, which includes theater.

▶▶▶▶ **FIND OUT MORE** ◀◀◀◀

British Isles; English Channel; English History; English Language; Industrial Revolution; London; Northern Ireland; Scotland; United Kingdom; Wales

◀ **Polperro—with its narrow streets and whitewashed houses—is a typical fishing village in south Cornwall, England. Villages such as this are popular tourist destinations during the summer.**

About 40,000 years ago, the first people moving into Britain simply walked north from the continent of Europe. The English Channel did not exist. Even after the sea separated Europe and Britain 9,000 years ago, Stone Age people could still travel back and forth quite easily. The Channel was quite shallow and could be forded.

ENGLISH CHANNEL

The British people call the narrow stretch of water between England and France the English Channel. Because of its shape, the French call it *La Manche* ("The Sleeve"). The channel has played an important part in English history for thousands of years. Today, it is one of the world's busiest water ways. (See the map with the article on BRITISH ISLES.)

The English Channel is 150 miles (240 km) wide at the western end, where it meets the Atlantic Ocean. It narrows to 21 miles (34 km) at the eastern end. Here it runs into the Strait of Dover, which links it with the North Sea. Resorts and busy seaports line the French and English coasts. The tides in the channel are strong and storms are frequent. Lighthouses and lightships help ships' captains to navigate the busy waters.

Since early times, invaders from continental Europe have chosen the channel as the best way to reach the English coast. Warships carried the armies of Julius Caesar to Britain in 54 and 55 B.C. A second Roman invasion, in A.D. 43, began more than four centuries of Roman occupation. The last invading army crossed from Normandy in 1066, led by William the Conqueror. The famous defeat of the Spanish Armada in 1588 took place in the English Channel. During World War II, Allied forces crossed the channel in airplanes and ships to begin the D-Day offensive (1944) that eventually ended the war.

Swimming the Channel between Dover, England, and Calais, France, is a challenge. First to make the swim was Captain Matthew Webb in 1875. In 1926, Gertrude Ederle became the first woman to swim the Channel.

Ferries carrying passengers and cargo cross the channel regularly. A railroad tunnel beneath the channel joins England and France. The tunnel is 31 miles (50 km) long and carries both passengers and freight.

▶▶▶▶ **FIND OUT MORE** ◀◀◀◀
British Isles; Engineering; France

▶ Miles of white cliffs can be seen from Beachy Head, near Brighton on the English Channel. The cliffs are white in color because they are composed mainly of chalk.

ENGLISH HISTORY

The first people living in what is now England came from Europe. They were Stone Age hunters who used stones to make tools and weapons. People later learned how to use bronze and work the soil. These Bronze Age people worshiped the sun. They moved stones great distances and put them into big circles, probably to form a place to worship. Stonehenge, the best known of these ancient circles, is still standing. The arrangement of the stones indicates that Stonehenge was probably also a kind of giant

calendar. The builders must have had a good knowledge of astronomy.

Other people, known as Celts, invaded southern Britain between the sixth and the first centuries B.C., moving there to escape from stronger European tribes. They made tools from iron, and they worked as farmers, cattle herders, and traders.

The Romans first invaded Britain in 55 B.C., and after a full-scale occupation in A.D. 43, they ruled it for over 400 years. They built many good roads, as well as fortified towns, such as Eboracum (now York) and Londinium (London). The Picts who lived in the northern part of the country fought against the Romans. In the A.D. 120s, the Romans built an east-west wall across northern Britain, known as Hadrian's Wall, to keep the Picts away. The Roman legions (regiments) gradually left the island after A.D. 400, because they were needed to defend other parts of the Roman Empire.

Early Government

The south, being the part of Britain nearest to Europe, was the part most easy to invade. Even before the Romans left the island, Angles, Saxons, and Jutes came from areas that are now southern Denmark and Germany. These *Anglo-Saxons* brought their families and settled in villages. Many English place-names are Anglo-Saxon in origin. The Anglo-Saxons were not the only people to invade. The Norsemen (Vikings) and the Danes first came in the eighth century A.D. The Danes later

▲ **Stonehenge in southern England was built between 3,000 and 4,000 years ago.**

gained control of much of the eastern part of England, though the English king Alfred the Great prevented them taking the rest.

At the time when the Vikings were invading the coasts of England, a young man named Alfred became king of Wessex, a kingdom in the west. At first Alfred was beaten by the Vikings and he was forced to go into hiding. While in hiding, he disguised himself as a peasant to avoid capture. During his escape, Alfred was offered shelter by an old peasant woman who did not know he was the king. One day the woman went out on an errand and told Alfred to keep his eye on some cakes that were baking on the hearth. But Alfred forgot about the cakes. He started to think how he could beat the Viking invaders. When the old woman returned, the cakes were burned to cinders. She was so angry she beat her royal guest with a pan.

◀ **Beautiful relics of the Anglo-Saxon era were found in the Sutton Hoo ship burial, excavated by archeologists. The burial may have been that of an East Anglian king, who lived in the 600s. The Angles and Saxons were farmers, warriors, and fine craftsmen.**

▲ The Normans charge on the defending English army at the Battle of Hastings in 1066. The Normans fought the battle on horseback, while most of the English soldiers fought on foot.

THE NORMANS RULE. The Normans, the last people successfully to invade Britain, sailed to England from northern France in 1066. Led

▼ Under the English feudal system, bishops and knights had authority, but peasants and foot soldiers held no power.

by William the Conqueror, they defeated the English king, Harold, at the Battle of Hastings. The Norman kings set up a *feudal system*. The king owned all of the land and gave large grants to a few people, called *nobles* or *barons*. In return for the land, the barons and nobles lent troops to the kings to protect them and fight battles. The feudal system lasted for about 200 years in England.

GOVERNMENT CHANGES. The problem with the feudal system was that the country was not firmly united. The barons often fought with the king and among themselves. The modern English government began to develop during the reign of King John (1199–1216). King John tried to make the nobles pay high taxes. The barons rebelled, and they forced John to sign a document called the *Magna Carta,* or Great Charter, in 1215. It said that the king, like any other citizen, must obey the law. The Magna Carta also limited the king's power and guaranteed that no Englishman could be put in prison without a trial. It also provided for a new system of law courts.

After King John died, the barons and the kings continued to struggle for power. The Magna Carta had indicated a change in government, and a new type of government gradually developed. The *Great Council,* established in the 1200s, was an early form of Parliament.

After Edward III (1312–1377) became king, he wanted to rule greater territory. When he found that his armies could not win Scotland, he tried to claim the throne of France. A war broke out that was fought, on

▼ **Henry VIII helped to establish a permanent English navy of 50 ships and about 8,000 sailors. One of the new ships he built was the *Mary Rose,* which capsized in 1545.**

and off, between 1337 and 1453. It was called the *Hundred Years' War.*

Shortly after the Hundred Years' War ended, the English went to war again. The new war was between two families, each of whom wanted its leader to be king. One family, the House of Lancaster, used a red rose as a symbol. The other family, the House of York, used a white rose as its emblem. The battles these two families fought thus became known as the *Wars of the Roses* (1455–1485). These wars ended when Henry Tudor, a Lancastrian, defeated and killed King Richard III. Henry Tudor married Elizabeth of the House of York and was crowned Henry VII.

ENGLAND BUILDS AN EMPIRE. Most English were Roman Catholics when Henry VIII came to the throne in 1509. Henry VIII

became angry when the pope refused to let him divorce the first of his six wives. He decided to break the power of the church. He announced that the king, and not the pope, would be the head of the Church of England. Under Henry's daughter, Elizabeth I, England became a prosperous world power. English ships sailed to all parts of the globe to explore and trade. The English navy defeated the Spanish Armada's invading warships, in 1588. Several of England's most important writers, such as Shakespeare, lived during this era. Ireland came under English control, and colonization was begun in Virginia.

James Stuart, king of Scotland, followed Elizabeth to the throne. He became King James I of England. He was already James VI of Scotland. So the two countries were united under one king for the first time. James and his son, Charles I, were not very popular. They believed that their right to rule was given to them by God. Many people did not agree with this "divine right of kings." Moreover, they were unhappy about certain aspects of the church. This group became known as *Parliamentarians, Puritans,* or *Roundheads.* Those who supported the king and his church were called *Royalists* or *Cavaliers.*

QUIZ
1. Who settled in Britain first—the Vikings or the Romans?
2. What important change did the Norman conquerors introduce into English society?
3. Which king signed the Magna Carta?
4. Who were the opposing sides in the Wars of the Roses?
5. Who was the longest reigning British monarch?
6. What countries make up the United Kingdom?
(Answers on page 1024)

▼ **A parliamentary Roundhead, mounted on a horse, confronts a royalist Cavalier in the English Civil War. The Roundheads wore plain, practical clothes**

THE KINGS AND QUEENS OF ENGLAND AND THE UNITED KINGDOM

THE ANGLO-SAXONS

Egbert	828–839
Ethelwulf	839–858
Ethelbald	858–860
Ethelbert (Aethelberht)	860–866
Ethelred (Aethelred)	866–871
Alfred (the Great)	871–899
Edward (the Elder)	899–924
Athelstan	924–939
Edmund I	939–946
Edred	946–955
Edwy	955–959
Edgar (the Peaceful)	959–975
Edward (the Martyr)	975–978
Ethelred II (the Unready)	978–1016
Edmund II (Ironside)	1016–1017

THE DANES

Canute	1018–1035
Harold I (Harefoot)	1035–1040
Hardecanute	1040–1042

THE SAXONS

Edward (the Confessor)	1042–1066
Harold II	1066

THE NORMANS

William I (the Conqueror)	1066–1087
William II (Rufus)	1087–1100
Henry I (Beauclerck)	1100–1135
Stephen	1135–1154

THE PLANTAGENETS

Henry II	1154–1189
Richard I (the Lion-Hearted)	1189–1199
John	1199–1216
Henry III	1216–1272
Edward I	1272–1307
Edward II	1307–1327
Edward III	1327–1377
Richard II	1377–1399

THE HOUSE OF LANCASTER

Henry IV	1399–1413
Henry V	1413–1422
Henry VI	1422–1461

THE HOUSE OF YORK

Edward IV	1461–1470

RETURN OF THE HOUSE OF LANCASTER

Henry VI	1470–1471

RETURN OF THE HOUSE OF YORK

Edward IV	1471–1483
Edward V	1483
Richard III	1483–1485

THE HOUSE OF TUDOR

Henry VII	1485–1509
Henry VIII	1509–1547
Edward VI	1547–1553
Mary I (Bloody Mary)	1553–1558
Elizabeth I	1558–1603

THE HOUSE OF STUART

James I	1603–1625
Charles I	1625–1649

THE ENGLISH REPUBLIC

Oliver Cromwell	1649–1658
Richard Cromwell	1658–1659

RETURN OF THE HOUSE OF STUART

Charles II	1660–1685
James II	1685–1688
William III (of Orange)	1689–1702
His wife, Mary II, ruled jointly with him until 1694	
Anne	1702–1714*

THE HOUSE OF HANOVER

George I	1714–1727
George II	1727–1760
George III	1760–1820
George IV	1820–1830
William IV	1830–1837
Victoria	1837–1901

THE HOUSE OF SAXE-COBURG-GOTHA

Edward VII	1901–1910
George V	1910–1917

THE HOUSE OF WINDSOR

(In 1917, the German family name of Saxe-Coburg-Gotha was changed to Windsor, the name of the royal residence near London).

George V	1917–1936
Edward VIII	1936
George VI	1936–1952
Elizabeth II**	1952–

*In 1707, the Act of Union was passed by the parliaments of England and Scotland creating the kingdom of Great Britain.
**In 1960, Queen Elizabeth II announced that her descendants will have the name Mountbatten-Windsor.

The English Civil War began in 1642, and Parliament beheaded Charles I in 1649. For a while, the Puritans, led by Oliver Cromwell, controlled the country as a Commonwealth (a form of republic). After Cromwell's death in 1658, many people became tired of the strict rule of the Puritans. Cromwell's son, Richard, tried to carry on after his father, but he was overthrown.

Charles II was restored to the throne. After Charles's death, his brother, James II became king. He was very unpopular because he was Roman Catholic. In 1688, the so-called "Glorious Revolution" took place. Mary, James II's daughter, and her Dutch husband, William of Orange, both Protestants, came to the throne as joint rulers. Before they were crowned, Parliament made the king and queen sign a bill of rights. The document limited the rulers' powers over taxation and the military.

The United Kingdom

The *Act of Union*, in 1707, made England, Scotland, and Wales one kingdom, called the United Kingdom of Great Britain. British territory and power also expanded rapidly around the world. The only setback in this expansion was the American Revolution in 1776. But Britain still held a huge amount of land in North America, which was later known as Canada. In the next 100 years, Britain spread its empire throughout Africa and Asia. During the long reign of Queen Victoria (1837–1901), Britain was the most powerful nation in the world. It was said that the sun never set on the British Empire, because it had spread to all parts of the globe. During this period, Britain became one of the most important industrial and trading countries in the world.

THE EMPIRE IN TROUBLE. In the early 1900s, trouble started for the Empire. Germany had been building up its own empire and a

huge army. This led to World War I. Britain, France, and Russia declared war on Germany and her allies in 1914. The United States entered the war in 1917 on Britain's side, and Germany was defeated the following year. The war was costly to Britain, not only in money, but also in lives.

Meanwhile, many Irish wanted Ireland to leave the United Kingdom. In 1921, much of Ireland became independent, except for six counties in the north that wanted to stay within the United Kingdom.

Germany had again become strong by 1939 and again wanted to become the leading nation in the world. Its army invaded Poland that year. This led to the outbreak of World War II. Many cities and towns in Europe were destroyed. For a time, Britain stood alone against the enemy. But eventually, Britain and its allies defeated Germany and its allies, Japan and Italy. Again the war cost Britain a great deal in money and human lives.

THE BRITISH COMMONWEALTH. After World War II, the British Empire began to change. The overseas territories in Africa and Asia wanted to rule themselves, as

▲ In 1851, Queen Victoria opened a great exhibition in London to show progress in science and technology. It was held in a huge glass building called the Crystal Palace.

▼ Queen Victoria reigned for so long that people speak of the "Victorian era." The queen is seen here in 1897 riding in a parade to celebrate 60 years on the throne.

▲ The Domesday Book recorded all the landowners in England in 1085, under the rule of William the Conqueror.

Canada and Australia already did. Britain did not want to hold on to its empire by force, so, one by one, new nations became independent and the Commonwealth of Nations was formed. Member countries are independent, but they work together in matters of trade and defense. In 1971, Britain moved toward a closer relationship with Europe, by joining the European Community. Although Britain no longer has an empire, or is a major world power, it is still one of the world's leading countries.

▶▶▶▶ **FIND OUT MORE** ◀◀◀◀

Art and Architecture see Big Ben; Cathedral; Constable, John; Reynolds, Joshua; Stonehenge; Tower of London; Turner, Joseph Mallord William; Westminster Abbey

Explorers and Exploration see Cook, Captain James; Drake, Sir Francis; Exploration; Hudson's Bay Company; Raleigh, Sir Walter; Smith, Captain John

Geography see British Isles; England; English Channel; Ireland; Island; London; Northern Ireland; River; Scotland; Wales

Government see Church and State; Commonwealth of Nations; European Community; Knighthood; Parliament; Prime Minister; United Kingdom

History see American Colonies; Boer War; Canada; Colony; Commonwealth of Nations; Declaration of Independence; Feudalism; Hundred Years' War; Industrial Revolution; Magna Carta; Revolutionary War; Wars of the Roses; Waterloo; World War I; World War II

Important People see Churchill, Winston; Cromwell, Oliver; Eleanor of Aquitaine; Grey, Lady Jane; More, Sir Thomas; Nelson, Horatio; Thatcher, Margaret; Wellington, Duke of

Kings and Queens see Alfred the Great; Arthur; Charles; Edward the Confessor; Edward; Elizabeth I; Elizabeth II; George; Henry; James; John; Mary; Mary, Queen of Scots; Richard; Victoria; William

Here are a few words that have come into the English language from other sources:

English Word	Source
alphabet	Greek
boom	Dutch
dental	Latin (dentalis)
Hallelujah	Hebrew
lake	French (lac)
patio	Spanish
piano	Italian
school	from Middle English scole, from Old English scol, from Latin schola, from Greek scholé
succotash	Native American (misickquatash)
their	Norwegian (theirra)
waltz	German (walzer)

ENGLISH LANGUAGE

When speaking English, do you realize you are using words from other languages, too? Many of the more than 500,000 words in the English language have been borrowed or adapted from other languages. Native American, Arabic, Dutch, French, German, Greek, Hebrew, Italian, Latin, Russian, Scandinavian, and Spanish have all contributed to the English language. Big dictionaries list the words in the English language and their meanings, and they also give the original *sources* of the words.

English has grown by many thousands of new words since its beginnings centuries ago. The forms and spellings and pronunciations of these

▲ The English monk Bede completed his book, the *Ecclesiastical History of the English People*, in 731.

words have changed greatly. Most changes in language take place so slowly that it is very hard to notice they are happening. But if you look backward in history from the 20th century, you can recognize these changes more easily.

The development of the English language can be divided into three periods—Old English, Middle English, and Modern English. These periods overlap, or blend from one to another. (1) Old English (*OE*)—also called Anglo-Saxon (*AS*)—was spoken from about A.D. 450 to 1100; (2) Middle English (*ME*) was spoken from about 1100 to 1450; and (3) Modern English (*E*) has been spoken since about 1450. Changes in English occurred in vocabulary, pronunciation, and *inflection*. (An inflection is a change in a word—usually in the final syllable—that shows the word's function within a sentence.)

Early History

The first people to speak the English language lived in Britain. Before A.D. 450, the people who lived there spoke a *dialect*, or version, of the Celtic language. Britain had been conquered in A.D. 43 by the Romans, who spoke Latin. The Roman soldiers left Britain after A.D. 400. Within the next century, the Britons were overcome by various tribes that came from what is now Germany. These Teutonic (or Germanic) tribes were the Angles, the Saxons, the Jutes, and the Frisians—all of whom spoke similar languages. The Britons' homeland came to be called *England* after the tribe of Angles. The language that slowly developed came to be known as *Anglo-Saxon,* or *English.*

Forms of English

The oldest form of the English language (OE) was based on the Germanic languages of those tribes that had conquered the Britons. A few Celtic words and many Latin words were kept, mostly military and com-

mercial ones used by the Romans during their long occupation of the country. Other Latin words crept into the language later. Many of these words were religious terms used by missionaries who brought Christianity to England. Other new words and word forms were introduced by the Danes and the Norwegians, who invaded England from Scandinavia during the 800s. Examine the lines from the long Old English poem, *Beowulf.*

De à wæs wundor micel/Dæt se winsele.
Wiotæfde headoderum...
Translation:
It was a marvel that the wine-hall withstood the battlers...

▲ **Before printing came to Europe in the 1400s, all books were copied out by scribes, which could take months or years to do. There was no paper, so parchment was used.**

The British writer George Benard Shaw claimed that, according to pronunciation rules of English, "ghoti" could be pronounced "fish." Sound gh as in "rough," o as in "women," and ti as in "nation," and you will see what he meant.

De mo ste dat in water is;
Dat tu wuldis sieien get,
Gef du it sog wan it flet,
Dat it were an eilond.
Dat sete on de sesond.
Translation:
The great whale is a fish
The most that in the water is;
That you would yet say,
If you saw it when it floated,
That it was an island.
That sat on the sea sand.

MODERN ENGLISH. As Middle English changed into Modern English, most of the old inflections were dropped. The meaning of a sentence began to depend on the *order* in which words appeared, rather than on the *endings* of words.

English is spoken by about 456 million people in the world. English is the *native language* (language of their country) of about 316 million of those people. They include Americans, Canadians, Australians, New Zealanders, some Irish, most British people, and some South Africans. People who learn English as a second language find it easy in some ways and hard in others. It is easy because it has very few inflections. English is easy also because it makes new words by joining two old words together: base + ball = baseball. Something else that makes English easy to learn: New words can be made by just adding beginnings or endings to existing words. These beginnings and endings are called *prefixes* and *suffixes*.

Some things about the English language, however, make it difficult to learn. The spelling of a word does not always agree with its pronunciation. Look at these six words and pronounce them:

      true who shoe
      blew zoo through

There are six different ways of spelling the same sound!

Some words have several different meanings. Look up these three words in the dictionary to see how many

▲ An example of an illuminated manuscript, written in the Middle Ages. The script is written in Norman French, the language adopted by the English ruling class in the Middle Ages, when the Normans invaded England. A banqueting scene, from the legends of Lancelot, is being described here.

▼ "Cent" and "scent" are examples of words in English that are pronounced the same way but have different spellings and meanings.

cent

scent

MIDDLE ENGLISH. The Norman Conquest of England in 1066 influenced the English language greatly. Since the Normans came from France, French became the language used by the English ruling class and for much written literature. Latin remained the language of the church, and English continued to be used by the common people.

This was the period of Middle English. The language absorbed some French words directly from the Norman. But since French was based on Latin, most Middle English words had Latin origins or beginnings. Because Latin itself had borrowed many words from Greek, English by this time had traces of Celtic, the Germanic tongues, Latin, Greek, Scandinavian, and French! It was, however, a language by itself because it had developed its own inflections, vocabulary, and pronunciations.

English had become the principal language of the ruling class in England and also of English writers by the mid-1300s. It replaced French in the English law courts and in Parliament.

Examine the lines from a poem, "The Whale's Nature," shown below. How is the language different from that in *Beowulf*?

Cathegrande is a fis

meanings each word has:

well interest pen

Many words are pronounced the same way but have different spellings and meanings. Do you know the different meanings of the words listed below?

capital, capitol
principal, principle
fair, fare
right, write

Idioms also create problems. An idiom is an expression, made up of two or more words, that has a meaning different from the sum of the meanings of its elements. It cannot be meaningfully translated word-for-word into another language. "Bite the bullet" and "blow my top" are examples of idioms.

American English

Since the early days when America was settled by the British, some noticeable differences have developed between British and American use of the English language.

Noah Webster, a young American schoolteacher, thought that common sense and convenience should determine how words are spelled. He tried to simplify the spelling of a number of English words when he was preparing the American Spelling Book (1783) and the American Dictionary of the English Language (1823). Today, Americans spell some words differently from the British.

British	American
cheque	check
humour	humor
travelled	traveled
metre	meter

Even greater differences in vocabulary exist. Some of the better known are these:

British	American
lift	elevator
petrol	gasoline
biscuit	cookie
chemist	druggist
underground	subway
subway	underpass

American English has also invented new words by combining two complete words or parts of them.

Two examples are:

sportscaster (sports broadcaster)
motel (motor hotel)

Pronunciation differences are also easily noticed. Americans pronounce more words according to spelling.

Every language has its own dialects or varieties spoken by people of certain groups or regions. "New England," "Southern," and "Standard American" are the three main dialects of American English.

▶▶▶▶ **FIND OUT MORE** ◀◀◀◀
Origin of Languages see German; Greek; Languages; Latin; Speech
Use of Language see Grammar; Language Arts; Limerick; Parts of Speech; Pronunciation; Punctuation
Written Language see Literature; Novel; Poetry; Short Story

ENGRAVING

SEE ETCHING AND ENGRAVING

ENVIRONMENT

SEE ECOLOGY

☼ ENZYME

Enzymes are substances produced by living organisms that make possible the process of breaking down and building up of materials in the body. Enzymes are all catalysts. A *catalyst* is a chemical that causes or speeds up a chemical reaction, but which is not itself used up in the reaction.

Without enzymes to work on the chemicals that make up our cells, life as we know it would be impossible. Enzymes are involved in every aspect of our body functions.

Enzymes are produced within living cells, and that is where most of

Listen to how you pronounce "Mary," "marry," and "merry." Most Americans think that these three words are *homonyms,* words that sound the same but have different meanings. British people, however, pronounce each of these words differently.

▼ **Enzymes have an active site, the "lock," which only certain molecules can "link" with, like a "key," to produce a chemical reaction.**

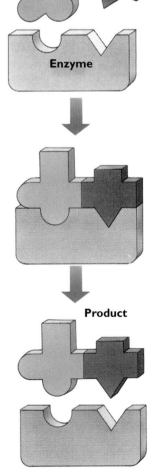

Molecules

Enzyme

Product

▲ Jacob Epstein, one of the most important sculptors of his time.

▲ Epstein's *An American Soldier*, National Gallery of Art, Washington D.C.

▼ A signboard marks the imaginary line of the equator, which passes through Kenya.

them do their work. Digestive enzymes are one exception. Such enzymes, which are often very complex compared to the simple enzymes that work within a cell, break down the food we eat into a form that lets it be absorbed by the body. Blood clotting is caused by another enzyme that operates outside of the cells where it is produced.

Many chemical reactions are always working inside any living thing. Injured tissue must be healed. Worn-out cells must be replaced. Food must be used to provide energy. And such processes must always be carefully controlled so that they do not get out of hand. All of these activities are controlled by enzymes. Enzymes start a process, other enzymes stop it, and still other enzymes continue it once more. Throughout a person's life, the body is controlled by the activities of enzymes. Without enzymes, none of the processes that are called *metabolism,* the chemical activities of the body, could take place.

An enzyme works by acting on a particular substance, combining with it, and changing it chemically. When it has done this job, the enzyme is released and is ready to go through the same process again.

Most enzymes act on only one kind of *substrate,* or substance. Each enzyme does very specialized work. So a large number of enzymes is necessary to control metabolism.

Enzymes in a system often work together as a group. One enzyme acts on a substrate. When it has done its work another enzyme goes to work, then another and another. The whole process is rather like a chain of dominoes falling over. The last domino, or enzyme, cannot work until the next-to-last domino, or enzyme, has done its part, and so on, all the way back to the first part of the chain.

▶▶▶▶ **FIND OUT MORE** ◀◀◀◀
Biochemistry; Digestion; Metabolism

 ## EPSTEIN, SIR JACOB (1880–1959)

Jacob Epstein's sculpture once caused a storm of angry protest. His work had a strength and directness that shocked people. Today he is recognized as one of the most important sculptors of his time. His work is still exciting, even though it is no longer so shocking.

Epstein was born in New York City of Russian-Polish parents. He became interested in art as a child and enjoyed making sketches of his neighborhood. When he grew up, he got a job in a bronze factory, where he learned to cast sculptures in bronze.

Epstein later studied art in Paris. One of his teachers was the great French sculptor, Auguste Rodin. Epstein also studied the collections at major art museums. He especially liked the primitive carved figures from Africa and ancient Egypt. His early sculptures were large, bulky figures carved in smooth stone. Parts of the bodies were exaggerated. His later work was modeled in clay and then cast in bronze. He would push and punch the clay to get a rough, rugged appearance that made the sculpture appear lifelike.

Epstein settled in England in 1905 and became a British citizen. He was knighted by Queen Elizabeth II in 1954 for his contributions to art.

▶▶▶▶ **FIND OUT MORE** ◀◀◀◀
Rodin, Auguste; Sculpture

EQUAL RIGHTS AMENDMENT

SEE WOMEN'S RIGHTS

EQUATOR

The equator is an imaginary line around the middle of the Earth. The length of the equator is 24,900 miles

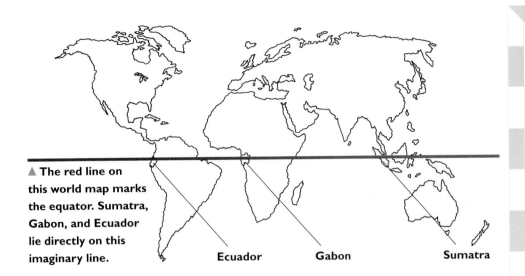

▲ The red line on this world map marks the equator. Sumatra, Gabon, and Ecuador lie directly on this imaginary line.

Ecuador   Gabon   Sumatra

EQUATORIAL GUINEA

Capital city
Malabo (15,000 people)

Area
10,831 square miles
(28,050 sq. km)

Population
351,000 people

Government
Single-party republic

Natural resources
No mineral resources. Forests provide some lumber

Export products
Cacao, coffee, tropical woods

Unit of money
Bipkwele

Official language
Spanish

(40,071 km). Until recently, people thought that at every point the equator was an equal distance from the North and South poles.

Space satellites can now make precise measurements of the Earth. The distance from the equator to the North Pole is a little longer than from the equator to the South Pole. The equator, therefore, is not really at an equal distance from the North and South poles at every point. This phenomenon is caused by the fact that the Earth is not perfectly round but is slightly flattened at the poles.

The equator divides the Earth into two halves, a Northern Hemisphere and a Southern Hemisphere. For most of its length, the equator runs across empty oceans. The lands it crosses are northern South America, central Africa, and the Indonesian Islands of Sumatra, Borneo, and Sulawesi (Celebes).

Most places near the equator have a hot climate, because the sun's rays fall directly upon the area. Manaus, Brazil, for example, has an annual average temperature of 81°F (27°C). It lies at an altitude of 105 feet (32 m) above sea level in the upper Amazon region.

However, some places at high altitudes near the equator have cool cli-

mates. Quito, Ecuador, located 9,250 feet (2,819 m) high in the Andes Mountains, has an annual average temperature of 57°F (14°C). The sun's rays fall at an angle on places farther from the equator. Most areas away from the equator have lower annual average temperatures.

EQUATORIAL GUINEA

The Republic of Equatorial Guinea has two parts. One is a small piece of land—about the size of the state of Maryland—on the west coast of Africa between

Pt. Europa
Malabo ✪
Luba   ▲ Santa Isabel Pk.
         9,869 ft.
         3,008 m.
BIOKO   Riaba
I.
Pt.
Santiago

Bight of Biafra

N
W   E
S

0   25   50   75 Miles
0   25   50   75   100 Kilometers
© 1994 GeoSystems, an R.R. Donnelley & Sons Company

GULF OF GUINEA

Cameroon and Gabon. This is called the Province of Mbini (Río Muni). The other part consists of two islands,

Pt. Epote
Ayamiken •   Micomeseng •   Ebebiyín •
Bata •   • Niefang   Abia R. •Anisoc
Mbini •   Mongomo •
                          • Evinayong Mbini R.
Cape San Juan •   Aconibe •
         Cogo •   Nsoc •
Corisco   d Elobey   Acurenam •
Bay   I.

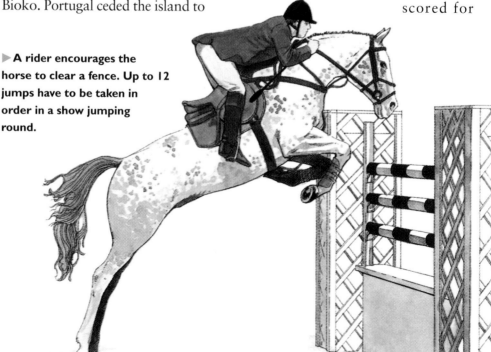

Bioko (formerly Fernando Póo) and tiny Annobón, a few hundred miles off the African coast in the Gulf of Guinea. This part is called the Province of Fernando Póo. (See the map with the article on AFRICA.)

The Province of Mbini (Río Muni), on the African mainland, is covered with jungles of huge ebony and mahogany trees. It has a narrow strip of white, sandy beaches. The climate is very hot and rainy.

The soil of Mbini is poor for farming. Most of the people in this province earn their living as laborers in lumber camps.

Equatorial Guinea's capital and largest city is Malabo, located on the island of Bioko. The island is made up of three extinct volcanoes, the highest of which is Mount Malabo, 9,868 feet (3,007 km) high. The rich, volcanic soil produces crops of coffee, banana, and cacao. Most of the people here are farmers.

In 1472, the Portuguese explorer Fernão do Po discovered and claimed Bioko. Portugal ceded the island to Spain in 1778. Freed African slaves were brought to Bioko in the 1840s. Bioko, Mbini, and some small islands were joined to form the colony of Spanish Guinea in 1885. The colony was renamed Equatorial Guinea in 1963 and became an independent republic in 1968. Thousands of people, including most of the European planters, fled the country because of the terrorism by the government of President Francisco Macías Nguema (1968–1979). After he was overthrown by a military coup, conditions began to improve.

▶▶▶▶ **FIND OUT MORE** ◀◀◀◀
Africa

EQUESTRIANISM

The Latin word for horse is equus, and an *equestrian* is a person skilled in many aspects of riding on horseback. Equestrianism as a sport is included in the Olympic Games. Horses and riders compete in a jumping contest over a course with several different kinds of fences. Fault points are scored for

▲ A horse and rider compete in a dressage competition. They must always be well dressed and groomed to give a good impression to the judges.

WHERE TO DISCOVER MORE

Krementz, Jill.
  A Very Young Rider. New York: Knopf, 1977.
Patent, Dorothy Hinshaw.
  Horses of America. New York: Holiday House, 1981.
Sayer, Angela. *The Young Rider's Handbook.* New York: Arco, 1984.

▶ A rider encourages the horse to clear a fence. Up to 12 jumps have to be taken in order in a show jumping round.

▲ In the cross-country event, horse and rider jump over obstacles such as wooden fences, hedges, and streams.

every fence the horse fails to jump cleanly.

Another equestrian sport is *dressage,* in which horse and rider are tested for elegance, discipline, and controlled riding. In another equestrian event, lasting three days, horse and rider must first take a dressage test, then ride around an open country course of fences, ditches, and ponds, and finally jump a series of fences. Equestrianism is popular in North and South America, Australia, New Zealand, and Europe.

▶▶▶▶ **FIND OUT MORE** ◀◀◀◀
Horseback Riding; Horse Racing; Polo; Rodeo

ERIKSSON, LEIF

SEE VIKINGS

 EROSION

Scientists believe that, millions of years ago, mountains as high as the Rockies towered over what are today northern Minnesota, Wisconsin, and Michigan. Only low hills are left now. The mountains were worn down by erosion. Erosion occurs through the action of running water, waves, wind, and moving ice.

In erosion by water, flowing water rolls, scrapes, and bumps small pieces of rock along the bottom of a stream or riverbed, and throws the rocks against the sides. The force of this movement knocks other small pieces of rock out of the bed, deepening and widening it. The current carries the smaller pieces downstream. This action goes on for millions of years, wearing down whole mountains and creating valleys and canyons as mighty as the Grand Canyon.

A raindrop is like a tiny bomb striking the soil and splashing it upward. Rainwater flowing over the surface carries loosened soil away. The best way to prevent erosion of soil is by growing plants in it. Leaves break the fall of raindrops, and plant roots anchor the soil and absorb most of the water. People who chop down trees to clear a piece of land, and then do not plant anything in the soil, are speeding up the natural erosion process. Fertile soil is washed away in a short time, leaving behind deep gulleys and poor soil.

Wind erodes the land by picking up grains of sand and hurling them against rocks. The hammering of the sand grains eventually wears away rock. In another kind of wind erosion, wind blows away loose topsoil that is not anchored by plants.

Glaciers are sheets of ice, sometimes 10,000 feet (394 m) high, that move like rivers. They erode the land by carrying along sand, pebbles, and large rocks. These eventually collect at the bottom of the ice. The sand and rocks act like sandpaper, scraping

The Dust Bowl is a region in the Great Plains where rain and wind eroded the rich soil because people used poor farming methods. During the drought of the 1930s, the soil vanished in terrible dust storms, causing many people to abandon their farms.

▼ This desert rock formation was created over thousands of years by the action of windblown sand. The erosion is greatest where the rock is weakest. The harder topmost rock is less affected.

LEARN BY DOING

To test the way ice can scratch and erode things, try this experiment. Ask if you may use the freezer to make some special ice cubes. You will need three ice cube trays, two bowls, two big spoons, sawdust, and sand. Fill the first tray with water, to make ordinary ice cubes. In a bowl, mix some sawdust with a small amount of water. Stir the mixture until it looks somewhat like oatmeal and pour it into the second ice cube tray. In another bowl, make a mixture containing a lot of sand and just enough water so that it looks like very thick soup. Pour the sand mixture into the third ice cube tray. Set the trays in the freezer.

When the cubes are frozen, perform the first test. Place one of each kind of ice cube in a saucer or a shallow pan. Which kind of cube melts first at room temperature?

Take one of each kind of cube outside. Which one is the easiest to break on the sidewalk?

Find the kind of plastic glass used at parties and often thrown out afterward. Which cubes scratch the plastic—the ordinary cube, or the special cubes? How does a sliding glacier work to cause erosion?

away the surface of the earth over which the glacier moves. Over thousands of years—as happened during the Ice Ages—glacial erosion wears down whole mountain ranges, making deep, wide valleys.

▶▶▶▶ FIND OUT MORE ◀◀◀◀

Canyon; Conservation; Ecology; Glacier; Grand Canyon; Ice Age; Soil; Wind

ESCALATORS

SEE ELEVATORS AND ESCALATORS

ESKIMO (INUIT)

Eskimos (Inuit) have lived for centuries along the coasts of the Arctic Ocean, in Greenland, Canada, Alaska, and Russia. Their homeland is a vast region, stretching about 3,200 miles (5,150 km) across some of the most thinly populated areas of the world. It is believed the Eskimos originally lived in Siberia, in Asia, and that they crossed the Bering Strait to Alaska. This migration took many years.

The Algonkian-speaking Native Americans originally gave the Eskimos their name, which means "eaters of raw flesh." The Eskimos of Greenland and Canada call themselves Inuit, meaning "men."

About 95,000 Eskimos live in Alaska, Canada, Greenland, and Siberia. Alaska's Eskimos include the Aleuts, natives of the Aleutian Islands. Among Canada's Eskimos are the Labrador, MacKenzie River, and Banks Island Eskimos. Greenland's Eskimos are split into two groups: the southern and the northern, or Polar, Eskimos. Siberian Eskimos live on the northeastern tip of Russia.

Eskimos are short and have heavyset bodies. Their round faces have narrow eyes and high cheekbones. Eskimos' hair is jet black, and the color of their skin varies from light to dark brown.

Eskimos hunt with rifles today, but they also use *harpoons* (spears) for hunting seals, walruses, and fish. Food supplies vary from one part of the Eskimos' homeland to another. Alaskan Eskimos have always eaten fish, as well as seal, whale, and berries. Eskimos living in northern Canada eat caribou, along with bear, some fish, birds, and plants. Many Eskimos now eat canned foods, packaged cereals, sugar, tea, and coffee.

Parts of animals not eaten are used for other purposes. From seals, the Eskimos make dog food, clothing, needles, tents, harpoon tips, and fuel for oil lamps. Caribou skins are used for clothing. Walrus tusks are finely carved, and animal skin is used for making canoelike boats called *kayaks*. The frame of the kayak is made of seal bones or whale bones. The Eskimos sew sealskin all around the frame. They leave an opening in the skin on top so that a man can sit in the kayak. Whale hunters use a larger open boat, called an *umiak*.

Eskimos call any form of shelter an *igloo*. The frozen snow houses we think of as igloos are used only by a

▲ Eskimos have flattish faces, with prominent cheekbones and straight, black hair.

◀ Eskimos cut a hole in the ice and catch fish with hooks and nets. They also spear fish that swim by. The Eskimo dogs in the background are hitched, ready to pull a sled. They are strong and able to withstand extreme cold.

few Canadian Eskimos. A snow house is made out of blocks of hard snow cut from the ground with knives. The Eskimos pile up the blocks to form a round house, big enough for one family to live in. These homes are warm inside. Eskimos living in Greenland make houses from stone. Alaskan Eskimos build homes from lumber. They once made turf houses that were partly underground. Summer dwellings are often tents, called *tupeks*, made from sealskin.

Eskimo dress is the same for both men and women. They wear waterproof boots, called *mukluks*, trousers, and a jacket with a hood, called an *anorak*, or *parka*. Women sometimes use their hoods as cradles to carry babies on their backs.

In wintertime, most Eskimos travel and move supplies on sleds pulled by dogs. The sleds have runners made from ivory, whalebone, or iron. When the ice covering the Arctic Ocean melts in the summer, Eskimos hunt seals and fish from their *kayaks*.

Eskimos are outstanding craftsmen. They carve walrus tusks into bird and animal forms. They also carve designs on the tools they make. Some Eskimos make wooden masks. These masks were once used for religious ceremonies.

When the Eskimos came in contact with white people, their way of life began to change. Eskimos were not immune to several of the white people's diseases. Measles, smallpox, and other diseases killed many Eskimos. The Eskimo language, which is understood by nearly all Eskimos, has changed. It now includes some of the white people's words.

Many North American Eskimos now live in towns and have abandoned their old customs. They find jobs in mining, construction work, fish canning, and at defense bases in the far north. Their children go to modern schools, learning to read and write English. But some Eskimos campaign to preserve traditional customs and skills.

> The Eskimos have their own kind of "ice cream." They make it by mixing seal oil and sometimes reindeer fat with snow and with berries that are in season.

WHERE TO DISCOVER MORE

Ekoomiak, Normee. *Arctic Memories*. New York: Holt & Co., 1990.

Jenness, Aylette. *In Two Worlds: A Yup'ik Eskimo Family*. Boston: Houghton Mifflin, 1989.

Yue, Charlotte. *The Igloo*. Boston: Houghton Miflin, 1988.

▶ ▶ ▶ ▶ **FIND OUT MORE** ◀ ◀ ◀ ◀
Alaska; Canada; Greenland; Native Americans; Newfoundland-Labrador; Polar Life; Russia

◀ A "modern" Eskimo on Southhampton Island (off the coast of Canada), travels around on a type of motor bike that is specially adapted to the rough island terrain.

ESTONIA

Capital city
Tallinn (482,000 people)

Area
17,375 square miles
(45,000 sq. km)

Population
1,573,000 people

Government
Republic

Natural resources
Oil and gas

Export products
Textiles, chemicals

Unit of money
Ruble

Official languages
Estonian, Russian

ESTONIA

Estonia was one of 15 republics making up the Soviet Union. It is about twice the size of Massachusetts and has more than 1½ million people, who speak a language similar to Finnish. Estonia is located on the eastern coast of the Baltic Sea in northern Europe. Tallinn is the capital of Estonia.

Estonia has a mild climate for a northern country. It is mainly low land, dotted with many beautiful lakes. It has extensive swamplands and forests. Along the Baltic coast are hundreds of islands, of which Saaremaa is the largest.

The soil of Estonia is very poor. The main crops are wheat and rye. Many farmers also raise pigs and cattle. Fishing, shipbuilding, mining (oil shale), lumbering, textiles, and machinery are important industries. In the past 1,000 years, the Estonians

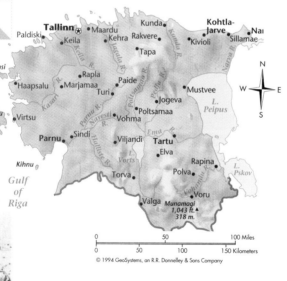

have been independent for only 22 years. The Danes and Germans conquered Estonia in the Middle Ages.

◀ **An aquatint etching, by the Spanish artist Francisco Goya.**

Sweden took over the area in the 1500s. Russia drove out the Swedes in 1721. Estonia became independent of Russia in 1918.

The Soviet Union took over again in 1940. The Germans invaded Estonia the following year and held it until 1944. Then Soviet rule was reimposed. The Estonians continued to oppose Soviet influence. In 1990, tension came to a head, and in 1991, Moscow finally recognized the independence of Estonia.

▶▶▶▶ **FIND OUT MORE** ◀◀◀◀
Russia

ESTUARY

SEE RIVER; SEACOAST

ETCHING AND ENGRAVING

Etching and engraving are ways of making a picture on a flat piece of glass or metal, called a *plate*. The plate is most often made of copper. The plate is then used to make a print on paper. Many prints can be made from a plate before it is worn out. Many famous collections of prints belong to art museums in North America and Europe. They are not displayed as often as paintings, however, because they fade easily.

Making an Etching
Etching is a technique similar to engraving. Artists cover a plate with wax, then draw on it with a needle. Wherever they move the needle, the wax comes off and the surface of the plate is laid bare. The plate is then put into acid. The acid bites into the plate where the metal is exposed, so the drawing is transferred to the plate. The picture is then printed like an engraving. The technique of etch-

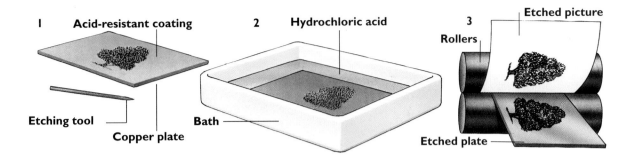

1. Acid-resistant coating Etching tool Copper plate

2. Hydrochloric acid Bath

3. Rollers Etched picture Etched plate

▲ How an etching is made: 1. The picture is scratched through a coating of acid-resistant wax covering a copper plate. 2. Acid burns the picture into the metal. 3. Ink is applied to the plate, which is forced through rollers with a sheet of paper to make a print.

ing gives artists much more freedom than engraving. It often allows them to include more detail in the print.

The Dutch artist Rembrandt van Rijn (1606–1669) created many beautiful etchings. A detail of one of his prints, *Christ Preaching*, is shown below. The lines and detailing of the print vividly portray the powerful personality of Jesus Christ.

The Spanish artist, Francisco Goya (1746–1828), used a different etching technique called *aquatint*. With this method, the artist could make not only etched lines but shaded patches as well. Many of Goya's etchings show his strong feelings about cruelty, lack of freedom, and stupidity. Look at the picture shown on page 938. In it, Goya makes fun of a young man in love—bowing and doffing his hat to a young woman who shows little interest. Two old women in the background gossip about them. The girl's *duenna* (an older woman who always used to accompany an unmarried girl in Spain) watches coldly.

Making an Engraving

To make an engraving, artists take a pointed tool called a *burin*, and cut a design into the plate. They rub ink over the plate, then wipe off all of it except the part that sinks into the lines made by the burin. They press a piece of paper very hard against the plate. The ink that has stayed in the lines is squeezed onto the paper to make the print. An artist must learn to handle the burin delicately and control the depth of each of the lines.

One of the greatest engravers of all time was the German artist, Albrecht Dürer (1471–1528). He was born in Nuremberg, the son of a goldsmith. Most artists of Dürer's time were putting beautiful, idealized people in their paintings and drawings. But Dürer drew people as he really saw them, and sometimes exaggerated ugly or unusual features. His engravings, often of imaginary scenes, are powerful and convincing. One of his most famous engravings is *The Knight, Death, and the Devil*. Dürer made this engraving as a plea to the Dutch philosopher Erasmus, urging him to begin reforms in the Roman Catholic church, which had become very corrupt.

▶▶▶▶ FIND OUT MORE ◀◀◀◀
Rembrandt Van Rijn

▲ *The Knight, Death, and the Devil,* an engraving by the German painter and printmaker Albrecht Dürer.

▼ A detail from *Christ Preaching,* an etching by the great Dutch artist Rembrandt van Rijn, who lived during the 1600s.

ETHIOPIA

Capital city
Addis Ababa
(1,495,000 people)

Area
471,778 square miles
(1,221,900 sq. km)

Population
50,341,000 people

Government
Republic (under military control)

Natural resources
Small amounts of undeveloped oil and natural gas, also platinum, gold, copper, salt

Export products
Coffee, oilseeds, hides and skins

Unit of money
Birr

Official language
Amharic

There are more people in Ethiopia than in any other African country except Nigeria and Egypt.

ETHIOPIA

Ethiopia is an independent country in northeastern Africa. It is one of the continent's larger nations—somewhat bigger than Texas, Oklahoma, and New Mexico combined. Ethiopia is a mountainous nation bordered by Sudan to the northwest, Kenya to the south, and Somalia to the south and east. The Red Sea forms the nation's northern boundary. The highest mountain, Ras Dashen, is 15,160 feet (4,620 m) high and located in the north. The great river named the Blue Nile, or Abay, begins in Lake Tana in the west of the country.

The climate is mild in much of the country where the altitude is high. But along the Red Sea coast, it is hot. The inland valleys and swamps are hot and humid.

The Ethiopians come from many different tribes, including the Hamitic and Semitic peoples of ancient times. Today most Ethiopians live in rural areas. The country suffers from periodic droughts, resulting in crop failure and famine. The main crops of the farmers are coffee, grain, cotton, sugarcane, and oilseeds. Small amounts of gold, platinum, rock salt, and other minerals are mined, and there are small oil deposits. Industries, such as food processing and textiles, are developing.

The kingdom of Ethiopia was established about 1000 B.C. by Menelik I, King Solomon's first son who was supposedly borne by the Queen of Sheba. "The Lion of Judah" was part of the Ethiopian emperor's title. From the time of Christ to A.D. 500, a powerful empire at Aksum controlled northern Ethiopia. Christianity was introduced by Coptic missionaries in the 300s. The empire fought a series of wars against invading Muslims and in the 1600s split into several small kingdoms. Not until the reign of Menelik II (1889–1913) was Ethiopia fully united.

Italy invaded Ethiopia in the 1890s and took over the Eritrea region, as a colony. (In 1993, Eritrea became an independent country.) Italy seized the whole of Ethiopia in 1935. British

© 1994 GeoSystems, an R.R. Donnelley & Sons Company

troops and Ethiopians freed the country in 1941 during World War II.

Ethiopia was ruled by Emperor Haile Selassie (1892–1975) for 44 years, until military leaders overthrew him in 1974. A one-party socialist state was established under Lieutenant Colonel Mengistu Haile-Mariam. In May 1991, rebel armies in the northern provinces of Eritrea and Tigre overthrew Mengistu's government. A council and president are presently governing Ethiopia.

▶▶▶▶ **FIND OUT MORE** ◀◀◀◀
Africa

ETRUSCAN

Before the Romans came to power in what is now Italy, an ancient people called the Etruscans lived there. They lived in the country of Etruria, the region of Italy now called Tuscany. The Greek word for Etruria was Tyrrhenia. Today, the part of the Mediterranean Sea that lies southwest of Italy is called the Tyrrhenian Sea.

Most historians think that the Etruscans came to Italy from Asia Minor around 1000 B.C. We know very little about these people. About 6,000 short sentences and names in the Etruscan language have been found on walls, statues, and vases. But so far, no one has been able to translate them.

The Etruscans built magnificent palaces and temples. Their underground tombs have beautiful paintings on plaster. They were skilled in making a black pottery known as *bucchero*. They created large and impressive statues of bronze, stone, and *terracotta* (baked clay). Etruscan jewelry was especially lovely.

Most Etruscans were traders and farmers. They became very rich and powerful and extended their lands. At the height of its power, about 535 B.C., Etruria covered most of northern Italy. It ruled Rome and influ-

enced the Roman way of life. With a strong army and navy, the Etruscans tried to conquer more land, but they were pushed back by the Gauls. In 396 B.C., the Etruscans lost a battle to Roman forces. Other battles followed, and by the 200s B.C., the Etruscans were under Roman rule.

▲ **The Etruscan people enjoyed music, games, and gambling. In this painting from an Etruscan tomb, lyre and flute players entertain guests at a feast.**

▶▶▶▶ **FIND OUT MORE** ◀◀◀◀
Italian History

◀ **The Etruscans left very little writing, but we can learn about them from their paintings and sculptures. This wall painting, from an Etruscan tomb of the 6th century B.C., shows a lively fishing expedition.**

▲ **The Greek mathematician Euclid laid the foundations of modern geometry.**

EUROPE

Highest point
Mount Elbrus in
Russia, 18,481 feet
(5,633 m)

Lowest point
Caspian Sea, located
in southwest Russia,
92 feet (29 m) below
sea level

Longest river
Volga River, 2,194
miles (3,531 km) long

Biggest lake
Caspian Sea, on the
Europe-Asia border,
169,381 sq. miles
(438,695 sq. km)

**Smallest
independent
country**
Vatican City
Total population
696 million people

EUCLID (about 300 B.C.)

Euclid was a Greek mathematician who lived in the ancient Greek colony of Alexandria, in Egypt. He is sometimes called the "father of geometry." His geometry textbook, *Elements,* has appeared in more than 1,000 editions since printing was invented.

Euclid's greatest contribution lay in the way in which he approached geometrical problems. His starting points were five *postulates*—statements that he had decided were true. Mathematicians have long accepted four of Euclid's postulates, but the fifth was never proved. Put simply, it says that two parallel lines will always stay the same distance apart, no matter how long you make them. A man named Riemann used a different postulate that says that all straight lines intersect. This "non-Euclidian geometry" was used by Albert Einstein in his Theory of Relativity.

King Ptolemy of Egypt once asked Euclid if he could not make his mathematics easier. Euclid replied, "Sire, there is no royal road to geometry."

EUROPE

Europe is the second smallest of the continents, after Australia. Some geographers do not classify Europe as a continent at all. They consider it the western tip of Eurasia. (They make up the name "Eurasia" by combining the two names, Europe and Asia). But the landscapes, history, and cultural traditions of Europe are quite distinct from those of most of Asia.

Europe is separated from Asia by the low-lying Ural Mountains. It is bordered by water on the other three sides. Its northern coast is washed by the icy Arctic Ocean. The Atlantic Ocean lies to the west. Arms of the Atlantic cut into the land, forming bays and seas. The Mediterranean Sea is an arm of the Atlantic. It is part of Europe's southern boundary. The Baltic Sea and the North Sea, also arms of the Atlantic, flank the Scandinavian peninsula in the north. The oceans and seas around the continent have many islands, which are all considered part of Europe. Some are large and fertile, like Great Britain. Others are small and rocky, such as those along the Norwegian coast. Some, like Iceland, are far away from the continent.

Despite its small size, Europe has played a major part in the history of the world. Modern Western civilization began in ancient Greece. Europeans were among the first people to travel and explore the world. They took their ideas about government, science, and religion with them. Thus, these ideas influenced people in places where Europeans settled all over the world.

The Land
Europe has four main geographical regions: the *northwestern* uplands, the Great European Plain, the central uplands, and the southern mountains.

The northwestern uplands are rugged, rocky hills that run through northwestern France, the British Isles, and Scandinavia. The coastlines of Norway and the British Isles are broken by beautiful narrow bays and inlets. These inlets are called *fiords* in Norway, and *firths* in the northern British Isles (Scotland). Iron and lead are among the minerals found in the rocky hills. In Scandinavia, the uplands are covered with forests of pine and spruce.

The Great European Plain lies south of the uplands. It starts as a narrow belt in the southeastern British Isles and sweeps eastward through northern France, Belgium, the Netherlands, northern Germany, part of Sweden, and Poland. The plain broadens to include Finland and Russia east of the Ural Mountains. Europe's longest river, the Volga, flows south across this region of Russia. It empties into the great saltwater lake known as the Caspian Sea. The Great European Plain is the most densely populated and the most fertile part of the continent. It has rich farmlands and forests of beech, ash, oak, and elm. Many of Europe's major industrial cities are situated in this region.

The *central uplands* are a belt of high, flat hills that include part of France, Portugal, and Spain, and stretch through central Europe to the

© 1994 GeoSystems, an R.R. Donnelley & Sons Company

Country	Area in sq. miles	Area in sq. km	Country's population	Capital
EUROPEAN NATIONS				
Albania	11,100	28,748	3,278,000	Tirana
Andorra	175	453	51,000	Andorra la Vella
Austria	32,374	83,849	7,614,000	Vienna
Belarus	80,134	207,600	10,260,000	Minsk
Belgium	11,781	30,513	9,881,000	Brussels
Bosnia-Herzegovina	19,736	51,129	4,355,000	Sarajevo
Bulgaria	42,823	110,912	8,995,000	Sofia
Czech Republic	30,452	78,864	10,362,500	Prague
Croatia	21,824	56,538	4,690,000	Zagreb
Denmark	16,629	43,069	5,141,000	Copenhagen
Estonia	17,375	45,000	1,573,000	Tallinn
Finland	130,129	337,032	4,971,000	Helsinki
France	211,208	547,026	56,342,000	Paris
Georgia	26,900	69,700	5,460,000	Tbilisi
Germany	137,744	356,755	77,754,000	Berlin
Greece	50,944	131,944	10,141,000	Athens
Hungary	35,919	93,030	10,563,000	Budapest
Iceland	39,769	103,000	255,000	Reykjavik
Ireland, Rep. of	27,137	70,284	3,509,000	Dublin
Italy	116,304	301,225	57,461,000	Rome
Latvia	24,711	64,000	2,681,000	Riga
Liechtenstein	61	157	29,000	Vaduz
Lithuania	25,097	65,000	3,690,000	Vilnius
Luxembourg	998	2,586	377,000	Luxembourg
Malta	122	316	351,000	Valletta
Moldova	13,000	33,700	4,460,000	Kishinev
Monaco	0.73	1.9	29,000	Monaco
Netherlands	15,770	40,844	14,927,000	Amsterdam
Norway	125,182	324,219	4,245,000	Oslo
Poland	120,725	312,677	38,064,000	Warsaw
Portugal	35,553	92,082	10,434,000	Lisbon
Romania	91,699	237,500	23,278,000	Bucharest
Russia	6,593,173	17,075,000	148,040,000	Moscow
San Marino	24	61	23,000	San Marino
Slovak Republic	18,934	49,035	5,287,000	Bratislava
Slovenia	7,817	20,251	1,950,000	Ljubljana
Spain	194,897	504,782	39,322,000	Madrid
Sweden	173,732	449,964	8,523,000	Stockholm
Switzerland	15,943	41,293	6,724,000	Bern
Ukraine	231,990	603,700	51,840,000	Kiev
United Kingdom	94,529	244,100	57,376,000	London
Vatican City	0.17	0.44	1,000	Vatican
Yugoslavia	49,364	127,886	12,468,000	Belgrade

One-seventh of the world's people live in Europe, the world's second-smallest continent. It has a population density of about 175 people per square mile.

The *southern mountains* are majestic, snow-covered ranges. Deep, flat valleys separate the mountain ranges. The valleys are dotted with towns and villages. Cattle and sheep graze on green pastures higher up the mountains. To the east, a great range called the *Alps* crosses Austria, Switzerland, northern Italy, and southeastern France. The Alps include some of the highest mountains in Europe. Two of the greatest rivers of Europe, the Rhine and the Danube, rise in the Alps. Farther west, a range called the *Pyrenees* forms a natural boundary between France and Spain. Evergreen trees grow throughout the region of the southern mountains. The whole mountain chain is also known as the Alpine system.

Climate

The climate of Europe varies from the cold, ice-bound northern regions to the hot, sunny lands along the Mediterranean coast. Many areas in between have a temperate climate—warm in the summer and cool in the winter. Most of these regions have enough rainfall to maintain rich farmlands and thick forests.

Animal Life

Many years ago, wild animals of many kinds roamed the forests and plains of Europe. As time went by, hunters killed off many of them. The remaining animals had fewer places to live as more land was cleared for farms and towns. Bison and wild boars have almost disappeared. Wolves, brown bears, lynxes, and wolverines are occasionally seen in some parts of Europe. But the most common animals today are foxes, rabbits, hares, squirrels, and deer.

The number of different birds living in Europe is also growing smaller. The continent once had large populations of eagles, wild ducks, storks, and geese. But now, skylarks, finches, nightingales, doves, and sparrows are

Czech Republic. These uplands are less rugged than those in the northwest. Rivers have cut deep valleys into the hills. The region has poor soil, but dense forests of oak, beech, and ash are found in some areas. Europe's largest and most important deposits of coal are found in the central uplands. Two major rivers of France, the Seine and the Loire, rise in the French uplands.

among the most common birds. The seas around Europe have many kinds of fish and seals. Pike, trout, and salmon inhabit lakes and rivers in many parts of the continent.

The People

Humans probably first came to Europe from Asia and Africa many years ago. Today, people throughout large areas of the continent share similar physical characteristics. Many northern Europeans have fair skin, blonde hair, and blue eyes. People of central Europe and the Alps often have brown hair and eyes. Many people living in Mediterranean countries have dark hair and eyes. Europe is divided into many countries, each with its own characteristics. There is no common European language, but many Europeans understand English, French, or German. Russian is widely understood in the countries that once formed the Soviet Union.

Europe is one of the most densely populated areas of the world. For many years, the land could not produce all the food the people needed.

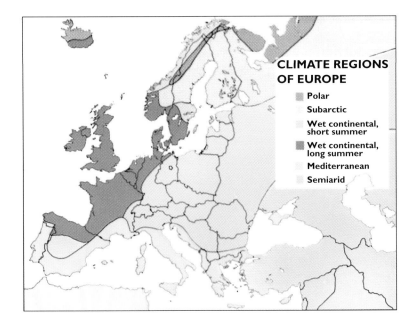

CLIMATE REGIONS OF EUROPE

- Polar
- Subarctic
- Wet continental, short summer
- Wet continental, long summer
- Mediterranean
- Semiarid

Today, modern farming methods make it possible to grow more food. In addition, ships bring food to Europe from other parts of the world.

As other regions of the world were explored, many families left Europe to make a living elsewhere. Other people left in search of political or religious freedom. Millions of Europeans came to North America. Many others went to South America, Australia, and Africa.

▼ **Beech and oak trees dominate Europe's temperate forests. Among the forest creatures, a polecat pauses with its catch, while a woodpigeon perches on a branch overhead.**

▲ An industrial area in the Ruhr district of Germany. Much of Europe is heavily industrialized. In recent years, there has been much concern about the effect of industrial pollution on the continent's (and world's) environment.

▼ Roman soldiers struggle against invading barbarians. The Roman empire began its decline when Germanic tribes increased their attacks on its borders in the 200s.

Europeans at Work

Europe is highly industrialized. Industrial development has been possible because the continent is rich in raw materials. A vast network of transportation routes has also been built up over hundreds of years. During the 1700s and 1800s, European factories became the first to use machine power, in the great series of changes called the *Industrial Revolution*. The most heavily industrialized areas are now in Germany, Great Britain, France, and Italy.

New agricultural machinery was also invented during the Industrial Revolution. Farmers found that they could grow more and better crops by using fertilizers. Belgium, the Netherlands, Denmark, and France became important farming areas. Major agricultural products include wheat, potatoes, sugar beets, vegetables, fruits, and dairy products.

The land along the mountainous coast of the Mediterranean Sea is not suitable for growing grain crops. But oranges, lemons, grapes, and olives ripen well on the sunny hillsides. Famous wines are produced from the grapes grown in this region and in other parts of France, Italy, and western Germany. The heavily forested lands of northern Europe are also unsuitable for crops, but these regions are famous for their timber.

History

The first great European civilization began in ancient Greece. The people of the Greek city of Athens originated the idea of democratic government. Greek artists, philosophers, and scientists left a rich heritage of knowledge and art.

Rome began to grow in power and wealth a few centuries before the birth of Jesus Christ. All of western Europe and the lands around the Mediterranean became part of the Roman Empire. Romans wrote strict laws for the government of this huge empire. Many modern countries base their laws on those of ancient Rome. The Roman language, Latin, became the basis of many European languages spoken today.

Belief in Christianity spread through Europe after the death of Jesus Christ. The early Christians were persecuted by the Romans, but the new religion attracted many con-

◀ This brooch of semiprecious stones set in bronze was made by an Ostrogoth barbarian in Spain during the late 400s.

authority in Europe. The power of the Church increased, and many people were converted to Christianity. Several European kings and nobles led expeditions to the Middle East to fight for control of the Holy Land. These expeditions, known as the *Crusades*, lasted from the 1000s to the 1200s.

By the 1300s, the feudal system was breaking up. Individual rulers were gaining control over large areas of land. The countries of Europe, as we know them today, were beginning to be formed. Trade between Europe and the Middle East had increased as a result of the Crusades. European cities grew larger, and merchants became interested in finding new trade routes. The Spanish and Portuguese were among the first to explore the coast of Africa, reach Asia, and sail to the New World.

The period of revival known as the *Renaissance* began in Italy before 1500. It was a time in which many new ideas in art, architecture, science, philosophy, literature, and politics developed. Members of the Roman Catholic Church began to disagree on various aspects of Christianity. One group of people, led by Martin Luther, split away from the Church during a period

▲ The ruins of an ancient Greek theater in Syracuse, Sicily. Signs of ancient times remain all over Europe.

Europe is named for Europa, a Phoenician princess in Greek mythology. Europa climbed on the back of a white bull, which leaped into the sea and carried her to the island of Crete. The white bull was really the god Zeus in disguise.

verts. In A.D. 313, Christians were granted freedom of religion. By A.D. 400, Christianity had become the official religion of the Roman Empire. Today, it is the most widespread religion in Europe.

Fierce Germanic tribes from central and northern Europe attacked the Roman Empire during the A.D. 300s and 400s. The Roman Empire began to collapse. The period of time between the destruction of the Roman Empire and the late 1400s is often called the *Middle Ages*. Kings and noblemen fought to gain control of the lands that were once part of the Roman Empire. Society was organized in a system known as *feudalism*. Under the feudal system, the nobles often became extremely powerful. One king, Charlemagne, built up a large kingdom in present-day France, Italy, and Germany. He was the first ruler to bring peace and order to Europe after the fall of Rome.

During the Middle Ages, the Roman Catholic Church was the only steady and dependable

◀ The spire of Ulm Cathedral in southern Germany is the highest spire in the world at almost 528 feet (161 m).

QUIZ

1. In which part of Europe did the idea of democracy begin?

2. Name three European languages.

3. According to the table on page 944, which is the fourth smallest nation in Europe (in size and population)? And the largest?

4. Name the mountain range that separates Europe from Asia.

5. If you look at a world map and follow the line of latitude nearest to Rome, Italy, west, where in North America will it lead you?

(Answers on page 1024)

▼ **A painting by Charles Cundall, showing the withdrawal from Dunkirk, June 1940, in World War II. More than 330,000 Allied troops were rescued from the beaches at Dunkirk.**

known as the *Reformation*. They formed the *Protestant Church*. For many years, Protestants and Catholics fought religious wars against one another.

Many wars have been fought in Europe. These have usually been between different countries, but sometimes, people within a country disagreed with their king or ruler and began a revolution. One of the most important revolutions took place in France between 1789 and 1799. The French king and queen were beheaded, and France became a republic.

France, Germany, Austria, Great Britain, and Russia became great powers during the 1800s and early 1900s. Their jealous rivalry led to the outbreak of World War I. This war lasted from 1914 to 1918, when Germany and her allies were defeated. During this period, a revolution broke out in Russia. In 1917, the Russians overthrew their czar (emperor) and set up a communist government. The Soviet Union was established in 1922. Peace did not last long in Europe after World War I. Germany and her allies fought other European nations again in World War II, between 1939 and 1945.

After World War II, Europe was divided into two factions, or *blocs*. The Soviet Union, Poland, Czechoslovakia, and other countries of eastern Europe were communist. The nations in western Europe were democratic countries. At the end of the 1980s, most Eastern bloc countries overthrew their communist leaders and established democracies. The Soviet Union broke up at the end of 1991.

Many western European nations are united with the U.S. in a defensive system called the North Atlantic Treaty Organization (NATO). An association called the European Community (EC), or the Common Market, has also been formed among many western European countries.

▶▶▶ FIND OUT MORE ◀◀◀

Cities see Amsterdam; Athens; Berlin; Florence; London; Moscow; Paris; Rome; Venice

History see Art History; Crusades; English History; Feudalism; French History; French Revolution; German History; Greece, Ancient; Holy Roman Empire; Industrial Revolution; Italian History; Middle Ages; Protestant Reformation; Renaissance; Rome; Rome, Ancient; Russian History; Spanish History; World War I; World War II

Languages see German; Romance Languages; Russian; Scandinavian Languages

Physical Features see Adriatic Sea; Aegean Sea; Alps Mountains; Baltic Sea; Black Sea; Caspian Sea; Caucasus Mountains; Danube River; English Channel; Mediterranean Sea; North Sea; Rhine River; Thames River

Travel see Big Ben; Leaning Tower of Pisa; Acropolis; Stonehenge; Tower of London; Versailles; Westminster Abbey

Organizations see European Community; North Atlantic Treaty Organization

Also read the article on each country listed in the table

EUROPEAN COMMUNITY

After World War II, much of Europe was in ruins. Several European governments felt that if the separate nations of Europe cooperated with one another, economic recovery could be speeded up.

In 1950, the governments of Belgium, France, Luxembourg, and the Netherlands began talks with the governments of their former enemies, Italy and what was then West Germany. These industrial countries first decided to pool their coal, iron, and steel resources. In 1952, they set up the European Coal and Steel Community, or the ECSC. Through the ECSC, coal, iron ore, and steel were moved freely from one country to another. Workers in these industries could also move freely.

The success of the ECSC led the six countries to set up the European Economic Community, the EEC, which was also called the European Common Market. The EEC came into being on January 1, 1958, as did the European Atomic Energy Community (or Euratom). Through Euratom, the six countries pooled their resources for developing nuclear energy for peaceful purposes.

The EEC worked to merge the economic resources of the six countries. It allowed the free movement of workers, goods, and *capital* (money). Soon other countries wanted to join. Denmark, the Republic of Ireland, and Great Britain joined in 1973, Greece in 1981, and Portugal and Spain in 1986. The European Community (EC) now forms the world's largest trading bloc. It buys and sells more goods than any single country.

The EC makes laws on such matters as farming, transportation, taxes, and food and health standards. It also helps other countries through special trade agreements or by making grants. The long-term aim of some people in the EC is to create a United States of Europe instead of a group of separate countries. But some people feel that this would damage their traditions and rights.

The EC is run by several different bodies. The 17-member Commission is made up of commissioners appointed by the member countries. But the commissioners act independently of their countries of origin. There is also a Council of Ministers. It is made up of ministers from the member countries. It can agree to or turn down proposals made by the Commission. The 518-member European Parliament advises both the Commission and the Council. If two-thirds of its members agree, it can expel the entire Commission.

▶▶▶▶ **FIND OUT MORE** ◀◀◀◀
Commonwealth of Nations; Economics; Europe; International Relations; International Trade

▲ The European Community headquarters building in Brussels, Belgium.

One of the EC's great problems is too much food. Europe's farmers are producing so much meat, milk, butter, and grain that huge stores of these foodstuffs keep building up at great expense to the Community. Scientists have calculated that Europe can feed itself in 50 years' time by using only one third of the present agricultural area. This is because of improved farming techniques.

EVANGELIST

A person who travels from place to place, preaching the gospel, or the teachings of Jesus Christ, is called an evangelist. Evangelists are also called *revivalists*. The meetings at which they preach are called *revival meetings*. Evangelists hope to bring about a revival (or renewal) of religious faith.

The first apostles traveled around, preaching the message of Christ and telling people about his life. They were the first to be called "evangelists." The Greek word *evangelion* means "good news," and these disciples were preaching the "good news about Christ." The written accounts of the life of Christ, by Matthew, Mark, Luke, and John, became the first four books of the New Testament. The word for "good news" in Old English was *gospel,* which is the name given to the writings of the four authors.

Most modern evangelists are Protestants. Evangelists may be either men or women. Some evangelists are ordained ministers. Ordained ministers have received intensive training not only in the principles and practices of their religion, but often in related fields, such as philosophy and psychology. Evangelists who are not ordained are usually called "lay preachers."

The British evangelist John Wesley founded the Methodist Church. Billy Graham is one of the best-known American evangelists today. He began his work in the late 1940s and has preached to millions of people throughout the world. Many of his revival meetings are shown on television.

▶▶▶▶ **FIND OUT MORE** ◀◀◀◀
Protestant Church; Wesley, John and Charles

▲ The British evangelist John Wesley, who founded Methodism. He preached his message in open fields, houses, and barns all over England in the 1700s.

▼ A map showing the Everglades, which stretch from Lake Okeechobee to the tip of Florida.

EVERGLADES

Southern Florida boasts the largest, shallowest, most unusual marshland in America—the Everglades. This flat, swampy region covers more than 5,000 square miles (13,000 sq. km). It stretches about 100 miles (160 km), from Lake Okeechobee to the tip of the Florida peninsula. Its swamps are usually only a few inches deep.

The soil of the Everglades consists mainly of peat. This is dark, rich soil formed by decayed plant matter. It makes excellent farmland when drained. The Florida government began work on draining the area in 1906. The Federal Government has also helped Florida to build canals and dikes for drainage and flood control. This work has made it possible to grow sugar cane and vegetables along Lake Okeechobee.

The southern part of the Everglades is now a national park. The best way to travel in the Everglades is in an airboat. An airboat is a flat-bottomed boat with an air propeller and a rudder like an airplane. Imagine that you are on an airboat piloted by a Florida ranger. As the boat gains

▲ The snowy-white common egret, found in the Florida Everglades.

speed, saw grass slaps the metal sides of the boat, then bends down in front as the boat rides along on a cushion of grass and water. Saw grass is a sharp-edged grass that can grow as high as 12 feet (3.6 m). The ranger sits in a high seat to see above the saw grass. Here and there amid this "sea" of grass you will see islands of soil, covered with tropical plants and trees, such as palms and gumbo-limbo trees.

In the Everglades, you can see wildlife all around. An alligator may be half buried in a mudhole, sheltered from the hot sun. Long-legged herons and white-plumed egrets look for fish to eat. Raccoons and otters play. Bass and garfish swim about. The small, hawklike Everglades kite feeds on snails, spearing them with its hooked beak.

Rangers spend part of their time searching for people who kill alligators. Alligators are hunted for their skins. In recent years, some 50,000 alligators were illegally killed in Florida. Stiff laws against poaching help to prevent this slaughter.

▶▶▶▶ **FIND OUT MORE** ◀◀◀◀
Florida; Swamps and Marshes

EVERGREEN TREE

If you live in a region where the winters are very cold, you know that many trees shed their leaves in the fall. Their branches are bare by the time winter comes. Trees that lose their leaves for the winter are called *deciduous* trees. Other trees have leaves all winter long, no matter how cold it gets. These are called *evergreen* trees.

Pines, spruces, hemlocks, and firs are among the most familiar evergreens. They are all members of a group of cone-bearing trees called *conifers*. Small pines and firs are popular as Christmas trees. The leaves of many evergreen conifers are called

needles, because of their long, narrow shape. The shape of the needles makes them able to withstand the low temperatures and harsh winds of winter.

Evergreens do shed their needles. But they usually shed them a few at a time, throughout the year, not all at once. New growth takes the place of needles that drop off. If you walk

▲ **The anhinga is a bird of prey related to the cormorant. It lives in the waters of the Everglades, feeding on frogs and fish.**

▼ **Conifer (cone-bearing) forests include pines, spruces and firs. These trees are hardy evergreens. Their trunks grow tall and straight.**

▲ **This evergreen magnolia is native to the southeastern part of the United States.**

Many scientists think that the course of evolution has changed from time to time because of catastrophes on Earth. Enormous meteorites, perhaps 6 miles (10 km) across, have struck the Earth during its long history. A violent collision of this kind would throw up a layer of dust so dense that the sun's rays would almost be blotted out. This would cause the Earth's climate to change enough to wipe out species such as the dinosaurs.

through an evergreen forest, you will see brown, dried-up pine needles on the ground.

Other evergreens do not bear cones and have broad leaves instead of needles. These evergreens usually live in places where winters are not very cold. Some types of live oak and magnolia that grow in southern parts of the United States are broad-leafed evergreens. Other kinds of oak and magnolia are deciduous trees. The American holly tree is found from Maine to Florida and as far west as southern Texas. The holly's shiny, dark green leaves and bright red berries are used to make attractive decorations at Christmastime.

▶▶▶▶ **FIND OUT MORE** ◀◀◀◀
Conifer; Plant; Plant Distribution; Tree

EVOLUTION

You probably have seen pictures of the huge reptiles called *dinosaurs,* or perhaps you have seen dinosaur skeletons in a museum. No dinosaurs are alive today. But like dinosaurs, thousands of other kinds of animals and plants lived for a time and then disappeared. What happened to them?

There has been a long chain of life from the first one-celled living things to the plants and animals of today. Why did some kinds of living things die out, and others survive? How did living things change from single cells to the complicated plants and animals of today? The answers to these questions make up the study of evolution.

Evolution Is Change

Evolution is a theory that tries to explain the origin and development of animals and plants that are on Earth today and were on Earth in previous times. Animals and plants that do not exist anymore are studied through their fossil remains. The theory of evolution includes two main ideas:

1. Living things change slightly from generation to generation. Over a long period of time, the offspring begin to take on new characteristics. This process has been going on for a very long time, and it has produced all the groups of plants and animals that have ever lived.

2. All living things are probably related, through ancestors they have in common. For example, evolutionists think that humans and apes probably descended, through millions of years, from the same kind of animal.

Have you ever wondered why so many different kinds of plants and animals exist? Many people have searched for answers. Since ancient times, thinkers have noticed that plants and animals change. None of them was able to suggest any reasons that agreed with the way nature works. Almost 175 years ago, a great French naturalist, Jean de Lamarck, put forth a theory of change in living things. His theory was made up of several ideas:

1. Part of a plant or animal can be changed by use or disuse. For example, a giraffe reaching for leaves high on a tree could permanently stretch its neck a little. The slightly longer neck could then be passed on to the giraffe's offspring. This is a change caused by use. On the other hand, whales came from ancestors that lived on land and had four legs. When whales took to living in the sea, they had no use for legs. Their legs, through disuse, shriveled away.

2. Animals and plants develop new parts that help them survive. If a giraffe needed to eat leaves that are on higher branches, then it had to increase the length of its neck in order to survive.

3. Characteristics acquired through use or disuse during the life of a plant or animal can be passed on to the offspring. Through many generations of use or disuse, changes resulted in new kinds of plants or animals.

First generation

Second generation

Third generation

Million years ago	Period	Bony fish	Amphibians	Reptiles	Dinosaurs	Birds	Mammals
2	Quaternary						
65	Tertiary						
145	Cretaceous						Mammal-like Reptiles
210	Jurassic						
245	Triassic						
285	Permian						
360	Carboniferous						
410	Devonian						
440	Silurian						
505	Ordovician						
570	Cambrian						
4,600	Pre-Cambrian						

CENOZOIC — MESOZOIC — PALEZOIC

Today, we know that Lamarck's theory was not correct. In some animals and plants, parts do not change, or *adapt*, to meet a new need. Many species that have died out might have lived if they had been able to adapt. For example, scientists believe that the world's climate changed about 65 million years ago, and that many plants died. The animals that fed on these plants also died because they could not find enough food.

▲ **The first vertebrates appeared about 500 million years ago, but mammals and birds evolved much later.**

◄ **Lamarck believed that evolution occurs when animals "improve" themselves over generations through effort. Darwin proved him wrong.**

▲ **Jean Baptiste Lamarck, the French naturalist.**

▲ The dark variety of peppered moth was once rare because it could easily be seen against a tree trunk and was eaten by birds. But natural selection has favored the dark variety, which is now dominant in industrial areas where pollution has blackened the trees, so it cannot be seen.

▲ A portrait of Charles Darwin at 31. He explained how living things developed from earlier forms of life.

We also know now that characteristics acquired in an animal's lifetime are not passed on to its offspring. If the tails were cut off 50 generations of mice, the tails of the 51st generation would be no shorter than those of the first generation. The change of a part is not assured.

Darwin and Wallace

The first reasonable theory of change in plants and animals was put forth by Charles Darwin and Alfred Russel Wallace in 1858. Darwin, after many years of study, was convinced that all living things came from common origins but had changed a great deal through millions of years. Darwin presented his ideas, along with a great amount of supporting evidence, in a book titled *On the Origin of Species by Means of Natural Selection*. His ideas caused other scientists to reexamine their own ideas about change in living things. According to Darwin, there are several explanations for evolution:

VARIATION. No two plants or animals are exactly alike. Among a litter of puppies, for example, one may have longer ears than the rest. Another may be brown, while the rest are black. Each generation has offspring that vary a little from their parents and from each other.

INHERITED VARIATIONS. Some variations that an individual is born with can be passed on to the offspring, and some cannot.

STRUGGLE FOR EXISTENCE. More animals and plants are pro-

duced than actually survive. Therefore they must struggle, or compete, with each other for food, water, sunlight, safety, and other vital things. Many die in this struggle. Only a few survive the dangers and live to produce offspring.

SURVIVAL OF THE FITTEST. The ways in which some individuals vary may give them an advantage in the struggle for existence. The advantage may be in getting food or escaping enemies. Plants and animals having these advantages will survive; others may not. If the surviving individuals can pass their advantage on to their offspring, the offspring will survive, too. These individuals are the fittest.

As a general rule, unfavorable variations are not passed on for many generations. Individuals having variations that fit them poorly for survival usually do not live long enough to have offspring. The disadvantaged individuals die out. As a result of the struggle for existence, nature weeds out the unfit and preserves the fit.

NATURAL SELECTION OF NEW SPECIES. Some changes in fitness may add up to large changes over many generations. Eventually, the changes make some individuals different enough to be called a new *species*, or kind. The individuals of the new species must be fitted for the struggle for existence, or they would not have survived. Since the individuals of the new species are different from their ancestors, the environment must have changed. The environment influenced, or selected, the new species through a process called *natural selection.*

Let us see how the process of evolution worked with the camel. Millions of years ago, the earliest ancestor of the camel appeared in North America. It was about the size of a jackrabbit. When it ran, it leaped, because its front legs were so much shorter than its hind legs. This animal eventually developed into a llamalike creature about the size of a sheep. During the Miocene Period, its descendant looked like the modern gazelle. This creature developed into the giraffe-sized camel of the middle Miocene (about 25 million years ago) and early Pliocene (about 13 million years ago) periods. By this time, the camel had developed a padded hoof for walking on sand.

During the Pliocene Period, these early camels migrated to Asia. There, over many generations, they developed other characteristics that helped them survive in hot, dry, sandy areas. The camel's teeth and stomach adapted to receive the dry grass and twigs available as food. It developed humps on its back to store large quantities of fat. In the desert, food and water are not always available, but the camel's body can break down its stores of fat into the food it needs. The camel's body tissues and pouches in its stomach help it retain water. The camel also developed several characteristics to protect itself from sand. It has two rows of eyelashes and hairy ear openings. And it acquired the ability to close its nostrils.

Other Scientists Study Evolution

Charles Darwin did not understand why or how variations in plants and animals occurred. No one else seemed to know. But just about the time that Darwin was presenting his theory of natural selection, an Austrian monk, Gregor Mendel, was finding the answer to how variations occur.

Mendel was carrying out breeding experiments with peas. He kept a careful record of the characteristics of parents and offspring of several generations. He was able to work out how many individuals in a generation would vary, and what variations might be expected. He showed that inheritance takes place in an orderly manner, and that both parents contribute equally to the characteristics their offspring inherit. Mendel published his work in 1866, but unfortunately, no one paid attention to it for more than 35 years.

▲ **Alfred Russel Wallace, an English naturalist, developed the same explanation for evolution as Darwin.**

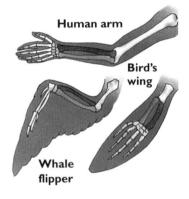

Human arm

Bird's wing

Whale flipper

▲ **The similarity of the bone patterns in a human arm, a whale flipper, and a bird's wing indicates to evolutionists that all three species evolved from a common source.**

Kestrel

Puffin

Curlew

Hummingbird

◄ **Birds evolved specialized bills to suit their feeding habits. A kestrel's hooked bill tears up flesh; a puffin carries many fish in its saw-edged bill; a curlew's bill digs into mud; and a hummingbird's bill reaches inside a flower.**

Irish elk

▲ **The Irish elk is now extinct, but other types of elk still exist, for example the American elk, which is better suited to its present-day environment.**

QUIZ

1. Were Lamarck's ideas correct?
2. Where did the earliest known ancestor of the camel first appear?
3. According to the theories of survival of the fittest and natural selection, which giraffe will live longest and probably produce more offspring: a giraffe with an average-sized neck or one born with a mutation that has caused its neck to be extra long?
4. Are genetic mutations good or bad?
5. What is the difference between chromosomes, DNA, and genes?

(Answers on page 1024)

956

A German biologist, August Weismann, showed that these inherited variations resulted from changes in sex cells (sperm or egg), and not in any of the billions of other cells that make up a plant or animal.

A Dutch botanist, Hugo de Vries, found in 1901 that small changes, or variations, can occur suddenly, in a single generation. He called these changes *mutations*. He found that some mutations were passed on to the next generation of offspring. He concluded that these mutations were the reason for new variations.

Natural selection then determines whether a mutation benefits an individual in the struggle for existence. And this, in turn, decides whether a mutation that can be inherited will be passed on to many future generations.

Scientists found that in each living cell there are tangled threads of matter. These are *chromosomes*. Each chromosome contains deoxyribonucleic acid (DNA), which is arranged in a number of very small units called *genes*. It is the genes that determine what characteristics individuals will inherit. The arrangement of atoms in the DNA molecule can be changed by high-energy radiation (such as X rays), heat, and chemicals. When these DNA atoms are rearranged, a mutation probably will occur in the next generation.

No one theory gives all the answers to the question of evolution. One of the most important facts about evolution is that all the facts are not known. What were our earliest ancestors really like? What fossils lie hidden and waiting to be found by a future scientist?

If you decide to work in this area of science, you might find the fossil of a "missing link," the organism that proves the relationship between one kind of organism and another.

▶▶▶▶ **FIND OUT MORE** ◀◀◀◀

Cell; Darwin, Charles; Dinosaur; Earth History; Fossil; Genetics; Mendel, Gregor; Paleontology; Reproduction; Wallace, Alfred

EXERCISE

Any activity in which we use our muscles is exercise. But exercise usually means activities that strengthen the muscles and improve health. Group sports, such as baseball, football, basketball, volleyball, and hockey, are excellent ways to get exercise and have fun. So are individual sports such as swimming, gymnastics, bicycling, or track. Social dancing, ballet, and modern dance all combine exercise with self-expression. Even taking walks every day is a good way to get exercise. It is better to have mild exercise often than to have strenuous exercise only once in a long while.

Keeping fit is an important part of good health. Many people follow a regular program of aerobics, a set of vigorous exercises that help the body process large quantities of oxygen. Oxygen-rich blood is necessary for the muscles to produce energy. All exercise helps the blood to circulate through the muscle tissues, cleaning out waste and supplying more oxygen than usual. The heart can then supply the body with blood more efficiently. Muscles become larger and better equipped to respond in an emergency

▲ **Jogging strengthens the legs, helps control weight, and improves the circulatory and respiratory systems.**

as well as to handle everyday jobs. A good weight reduction program should include exercise as well as dieting. Regular exercise makes relaxation and sound, healthy sleep easier.

Some people do exercises called *calisthenics*, which are movements designed to strengthen specific muscles. *Isometrics* is a type of calisthenics in which muscles are strengthened by using them against each other or against an object that will not move, such as a wall or door frame. Try this isometric exercise: Raise your arms to shoulder height. Press the palms of your hands together. Press *hard*. You should feel the muscles in your arms and shoulders working. Professional athletes do calisthenics to keep in shape. Calisthenics are also useful for people who do not participate in sports or other physical activities. Many other people like to exercise by *jogging*, running at an easy pace.

▶▶▶▶ FIND OUT MORE ◀◀◀◀
Circulatory System; Dance;
Gymnastics; Health; Muscle; Sports

EXPLORATION

When a famous person was asked why he wished to climb Mount Everest, he replied, "Because it is there." There have always been *explorers,* persons who go where only a few or no persons have gone before and see what only a few or no persons have ever seen.

People like to explore for many reasons: They may be curious and adventurous, or perhaps they hope to find something that will increase their wealth. Early cave dwellers often ventured into new territory in their constant search for food. Today, although many people know how to obtain the material goods they need, they are still excited by the unknown. Exploration is still one of the great adventures known to humankind.

Early Exploration
We have no written records of early explorations, but historians know explorers of long ago must have been just as brave and imaginative as today's astronauts who explore outer space. In early times, people knew so much less about the world around them that every new step into strange lands seemed a dangerous adventure.

The first known explorer who left records of his adventures was an Egyptian named Hannu. Hannu built a wooden ship and sailed south from Egypt along the Red Sea around 2750 B.C. He then traveled overland to central Africa. Hannu returned to Egypt in triumph with a cargo of monkeys, precious metals, incense, and tropical woods never before seen in his country.

The first seagoing boats were so light and fragile that they could be sailed only in mild weather, by day, and crews had to spend the night ashore. About 1,000 years before the birth of Christ, a remarkable people called the Phoenicians founded a nation at the eastern end of the Mediterranean. They used the strong wood from the great cedar trees of Lebanon and built the first real long-range ships. The Phoenicians set out to discover and trade with all the other civilizations they could find. They established colonies as far away as Britain and may even have sailed around Africa.

▲ Thor Heyerdahl, a Norwegian and modern-day explorer, set out to prove that early vessels could have made spectacular voyages. His ship RA II, which was made from reeds, sailed across the Atlantic.

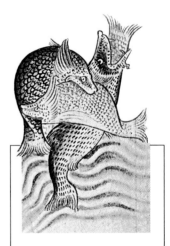

Sailing in the Middle Ages was an unknown and frightening experience. Sailors were terrified of what they might meet in unknown waters. They believed that huge sea monsters lurked in the deep Atlantic Ocean.

▲ A Viking coin, dating from the 800s. The Vikings traveled great distances in small ships to trade with Arabs in the cities of Baghdad and Constantinople.

WHERE TO DISCOVER MORE

Jackson, Donald Dale. *The Explorers.* Alexandria, Virginia: Time-Life Books, 1983.

Simon, Charnan. *The World's Great Explorers.* Chicago: Childrens Press, 1990.

▶ A section from a map made for the French king, Charles V, in about 1375. Travelers during the Middle Ages had few good maps. With the increase in trade, however, the need for maps grew. This map gives information about central Asia and China.

The Greeks built a cultured and advanced civilization centuries before the birth of Christ. Some of the most adventurous Greek traders may have dared to travel very long distances out into the Atlantic Ocean. Alexander the Great, in the 330s and 320s B.C., explored and conquered all of the Middle East as far as India.

The Roman Empire was founded not so much by explorers as by mighty generals. The Romans extended their holdings to include most of Europe, the Middle East, and North Africa. After the Roman Empire was overrun by barbarian tribes, however, a period called the "Middle Ages" began. Few expeditions set out from Europe for the next thousand years.

The Middle Ages

Exploration continued, however, in other parts of the world. Great empires existed in Africa, particularly in the western part. These empires were built up by imaginative explorers and maintained by lively caravan trade.

In Asia, too, there were probably a number of daring discoverers, although no known written history remains of their accomplishments. Most historians believe that the Indians of both North and South America originally came from Asia. Their ancestors must have been very brave explorers to risk crossing the icy wastes of Siberia and Alaska in search of warmer lands.

In Europe, the Vikings of Norway were the first to revive exploration. Recent discoveries in Newfoundland show that the Vikings had established an advanced colony there by about A.D. 1000 but soon abandoned it.

The Great Age of Exploration

By A.D. 1200, towns and cities in Europe were growing and with them came new wealth. A class of merchants developed. Contact with the

▲ Admiral Zheng He of China built huge ships for his expeditions in the 1400s.

East began during the Crusades. A young Italian, Marco Polo, journeyed in caravans across Asia to China and became a close friend of the Emperor Kublai Khan. When Marco Polo returned to Europe, the

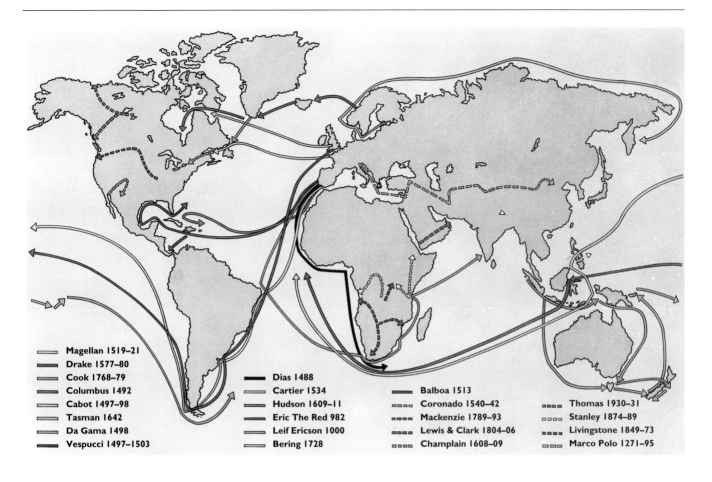

▭ Magellan 1519–21		
▬ Drake 1577–80		
▭ Cook 1768–79		
▬ Columbus 1492		
▬ Cabot 1497–98		
▬ Tasman 1642		
▬ Da Gama 1498		
▬ Vespucci 1497–1503		

▬ Dias 1488	▬ Balboa 1513		
▭ Cartier 1534	▭ Coronado 1540–42	▭ Thomas 1930–31
▬ Hudson 1609–11	▭ Mackenzie 1789–93	▭ Stanley 1874–89
▬ Eric The Red 982	▭ Lewis & Clark 1804–06	▭ Livingstone 1849–73
▬ Leif Ericson 1000	▭ Champlain 1608–09	▭ Marco Polo 1271–95
▬ Bering 1728		

FAMOUS EXPLORERS

Explorer/Country	Area Explored	Date	Explorer	Area Explored	Date
Erik the Red (Norway)	Discovered Greenland (s.w. coast).	about 982	René-Robert Cavelier La Salle (France)	Explored the Mississippi River to its mouth.	1682
Leif Eriksson (Iceland)	Probably the first European to reach North America.	about 1000	James Cook (England)	Explored and mapped South Pacific, including eastern coast of Australia.	1768–79
Marco Polo (Italy)	Far East including India and China.	1271–95	Alexander Mackenzie (Scotland)	Discovered Mackenzie River and explored western Canada.	1789–93
Bartholomeu Dias (Portugal)	First European to round the Cape of Good Hope.	1488	Meriwether Lewis and William Clark (U.S.)	Explored Northwest Territory over the Rocky Mountains to Pacific Ocean	1804–06
Christopher Columbus (Italy)	Discovered America, opening the New World to all of Europe.	1492	David Livingstone (Scotland)	Discovered Zambezi River and Victoria Falls and explored South Africa.	1849–73
John Cabot (Italy)	East coast of Canada, and east and west coasts of Greenland. Discovered Newfoundland.	1497–98	Henry Stanley (Wales)	Found correct source of the Nile River and explored Congo River region.	1874–89
Vasco da Gama (Portugal)	First European to reach India by sea.	1498	Robert Peary (U.S.)	Led first expedition to North Pole	1908–09
Amerigo Vespucci (Italy)	Made several voyages to the New World, after Columbus. America was named after him.	1497–1503	Roald Amundsen (Norway)	First to reach South Pole. Flew over North Pole in a dirigible with Umberto Nobile and Lincoln Ellsworth.	1911
Vasco Núñez de Balboa (Spain)	Crossed Isthmus of Panama and discovered the Pacific Ocean.	1513	Richard E. Byrd (U.S.)	First to fly over North Pole in a plane.	1926
Ferdinand Magellan (Portugal)	Commanded first voyage around the globe, sailing westward.	1519–21	Edmund Hillary (New Zealand) and Tenzing Norgay (Nepal)	First to reach the summit of Mount Everest, on border of Nepal and Tibet.	1953
Jacques Cartier (France)	Explored the St. Lawrence River	1534	Vivian Fuchs (England)	Led first completely overland crossing of Antarctica.	1957–58
Francisco Vasquez de Coronado (Spain)	Traced Colorado River northward, discovering Grand Canyon. Explored southwestern states and eastern Kansas.	1540–42	Jacques Piccard (France) and Donald Walsh (U.S.)	Made record 35,800-foot (10,900-m) dive in bathyscaphe in Mariana Trench in the Pacific.	1960
Sir Francis Drake (England)	First Englishman to sail around the world.	1577–80	Yuri Gagarin (former U.S.S.R)	First man in space.	1961
Samuel de Champlain (France)	Founded Quebec City and discovered Lake Champlain.	1608–09	Valentina Tereshkova (former U.S.S.R.)	First woman in space.	1963
Henry Hudson (England)	Hudson River, Bay, and Strait.	1609–11	Neil Armstrong and Edwin Aldrin (U.S.)	First men to explore the moon.	1969
Abel Janszoon Tasman (Netherlands)	Discovered New Zealand and Tasmania.	1642			
Jacques Marquette and Louis Joliet (France)	Explored northern Mississippi River Valley.	1673			

▲ In the 1400s, the Portuguese developed the caravel—a small, reliable ship for long sea voyages.

Columbus reached the West Indies in 1492. His Spanish masters, Isabella and Ferdinand, knew that the Portuguese were trying to reach the riches of the east by sailing around Africa. They appealed to Pope Alexander VI, asking him to divide the "unknown" world fairly between Spain and Portugal. This the Pope did. He drew an imaginary line 350 miles (580 km) west of the Azores islands, giving Spain rights to everything west of the line and Portugal rights to the east of it. In return, he expected Spain and Portugal to convert the peoples of their new lands to Christianity.

story of his discoveries and of the wealth of the Orient slowly began to create great interest in Asia.

Europeans came to realize that a mighty civilization existed in China, with a wealth of silks, jewels, and other exotic treasures unknown in the West. Spices from southern Asia could be used to flavor and preserve food. Trade between Europe and the East quickly followed. Ships sailed to the eastern end of the Mediterranean. Then, traders traveled by caravan across Asia. Many Italian cities soon became wealthy from this trade and gained control of the traffic in the Mediterranean Sea. Nations bordering on the Atlantic, such as Spain and Portugal, were determined to find a sea route to Asia.

Prince Henry of Portugal is known as "the discoverer of discoverers" because he encouraged explorers, and he promoted advances in ship construction and navigation. Under Henry's inspiration, Bartholomeu Dias sailed to the southern tip of Africa in 1488. Vasco da Gama followed Dias's route ten years later and continued on to India.

Christopher Columbus opened up a whole new wave of exploration in 1492 when he discovered the new lands

that lay to the west across the Atlantic. A host of followers explored the Americas. The Italian John Cabot was the first to reach what is now Canada, and Jacques Cartier came soon afterward, exploring the St. Lawrence. Giovanni da Verrazano, Captain John Smith, Sir Walter Raleigh, and Henry Hudson explored various parts of the eastern seaboard of what is now the United States.

The French explorers, Louis Joliet and Jacques Marquette, discovered the headwaters of the Mississippi, and Sieur de La Salle explored that river to its mouth. Antoine Cadillac founded Detroit and was governor of Louisiana. Hernando de Soto was the first to penetrate what is now the southern United States. The black adventurer, Estevanico, discovered the vast lands of what would become Texas and Arizona. His explorations paved the way for Francisco Coronado's discoveries in the southwestern United States.

▼ Captain James Cook's voyages of exploration took him to Oceania. In New Zealand, he was met by the Maoris, who rode in swift war canoes.

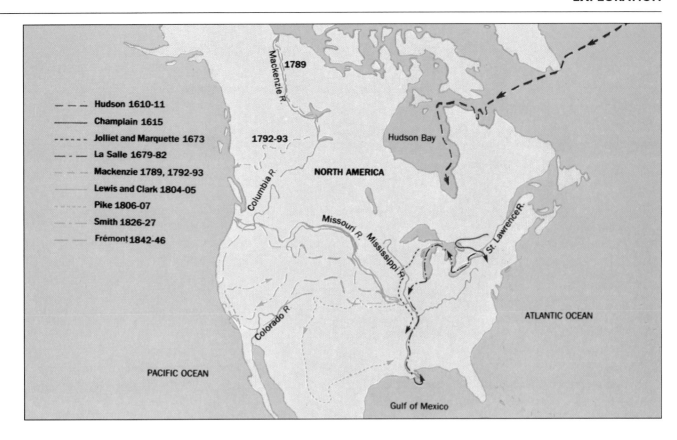

Hudson 1610-11
Champlain 1615
Jolliet and Marquette 1673
La Salle 1679-82
Mackenzie 1789, 1792-93
Lewis and Clark 1804-05
Pike 1806-07
Smith 1826-27
Frémont 1842-46

1789

Mackenzie R.

1792-93

Columbia R.

Hudson Bay

NORTH AMERICA

Missouri R. Mississippi R.

St. Lawrence R.

Colorado R.

ATLANTIC OCEAN

PACIFIC OCEAN

Gulf of Mexico

In 1513, Vasco Balboa crossed Panama and discovered that the Pacific Ocean lay beyond. Many people still believed that Asia could not be far away. Between 1519 and 1521, Ferdinand Magellan led an expedition that sailed around the world. People began to understand the true size of the earth for the first time—particularly the large size of the Americas and the Pacific. It took Magellan's expedition three long and desperate years to circumnavigate the globe. Astronauts now orbit the Earth in little more than 90 minutes!

The English explorer, Sir Francis Drake, followed the route that Magellan's ships had sailed. Captain James Cook continued the exploration of the South Pacific. In the North, the Danish explorer, Vitus Bering, mapped the treacherous reaches of the Siberian Arctic and Alaska.

Modern Exploration

The coldest parts of the world, the Arctic and Antarctic, were not explored until the 1900s. Rear Admiral Robert Peary of the U.S. Navy, traveling by dog team, reached the North Pole in 1909. Roald Amundsen, a Norwegian explorer, beat an Englishman, Robert Scott, in a race to the South Pole in 1911. In 1958, the U.S. nuclear submarine *Nautilus* sailed across the Arctic Ocean entirely under the water and passed beneath the North Pole 400 feet (120 m) under the ice.

The age of exploration is not over. Indeed, in many areas it is just beginning. The depths of the ocean still hold many challenges. In 1960, Jacques Piccard and U.S. Navy Lieutenant Donald Walsh descended almost 7 miles (11 km) to the bottom of the Pacific in a pressurized capsule called a *bathyscaphe*. The peaks of many high mountains remain to be reached. In 1953, Sir Edmund Hillary and Tenzing Norgay reached the summit of the world's highest peak, Mount Everest, but not before 11 unsuccessful attempts had been made to conquer it. Everest is almost 6 miles (10 km) high. Three Americans—Max Anderson, Ben Abruzzo, and Larry Newman—made the first trans-Atlantic balloon flight in 1978.

▲ A map of North America shows the routes taken by European explorers between 1610 and 1846.

▲ In 1909, the American explorer Robert E. Peary became the first person to reach the Earth's North Pole.

On April 30, 1978, Naomi Uemura, a Japanese explorer, became the first person to reach the North Pole alone.

▶ **Edmund Hillary of New Zealand and Tenzing Norgay of Nepal became the first people to reach the summit of Mount Everest, the world's highest mountain.**

In November 1983, a U.S. space shuttle carried *Spacelab* into orbit for the first time. *Spacelab* is a manned space laboratory designed by the European Space Agency (ESA). Up to four scientists can conduct experiments in a weightless environment while the laboratory rests in the shuttle's open payload area.

That same year, Naomi James of the United Kingdom became the first woman to sail alone around the world, and Naomi Uemura of Japan became the first person to make a solo journey to the North Pole.

Space Exploration

Space is perhaps the most exciting challenge for explorers. When the American astronaut Neil Armstrong became the first human to set foot on the surface of the moon in 1969, he declared, "That's one small step for a man, one giant leap for mankind." The Apollo moon landings marked the beginning of a whole new era of exploration. Even 25 years earlier, the idea of space travel still lay in the realms of science fiction.

In 1976, new discoveries were made about the planet Mars when two unmanned U.S. Viking space-craft landed on the planet's surface. Our vision was extended farther in 1979 and 1980, when another unmanned U.S. spacecraft, *Voyager* 1, flew by Jupiter and Saturn. A sister spacecraft, *Voyager 2*, revealed some of the mysteries of Uranus when it passed the planet in 1986. *Voyager 2* flew close to Neptune in August 1989, sending back pictures of the planet and its largest moon, Triton. The unmanned *Galileo* spacecraft was launched from the space shuttle *Atlantis* in October 1989 on a six-year voyage to Jupiter.

The discoveries of the 2000s will probably make the mighty explorations of the 1900s and all past ages seem minor by comparison.

▶▶▶▶ **FIND OUT MORE** ◀◀◀◀

Explorers see Balboa, Vasco Nunez de; Bering, Vitus; Cabot, John and Sebastian; Cartier, Jacques; Columbus, Christopher; Cook, Captain James; Coronado, Francisco; Cortes Hernando; de Soto, Hernando; Dias, Bartholomeu; Drake, Sir Francis; Estevanico; Gama, Vasco da; Hillary, Sir Edmund; Hudson, Henry; La Salle, Sieur De; Magellan, Ferdinand; Marquette, Jacques and Joliet, Louis; Peary, Robert; Pizarro, Francisco; Polo, Marco; Raleigh, Sir Walter; Verrazano, Giovanni da; Vikings
Geography see Africa; Antarctica; Arctic; Asia; Atlantic Ocean; Himalayas; North America; North Pole; Northwest Passage; Ocean; Pacific Ocean; South America
History see Alexander the Great; Carthage; China; Egypt, Ancient; Greece, Ancient; Henry The Navigator; Native Americans; Navigation; Phoenicia; Pocahontas; Rome, Ancient; Ships and Shipping
Space Exploration see Armstrong, Neil; Astronaut; Moon; Space; Space Research; Space Travel

▼ **Edward H. White II was the first American astronaut to climb outside an orbiting spacecraft. His "space walk" took place in June 1965.**

⚙ EXPLOSIVES

A pioneer farmer would spend a whole morning chopping away a large tree stump. Today, it takes a farmer five minutes to shatter a stump with an explosive.

An explosive is a substance that very quickly—in a few millionths of a second—produces a great amount of energy in the form of heat and expanding gas. The gas expands to a volume hundreds of times as big as the explosive. The gas travels outward at a very high speed from where the explosion has occurred. It is this high-speed, expanding volume of gas that causes explosives to have so much force.

Explosives are used in almost all weapons of modern warfare. Many kinds of explosives are used in peaceful activities, such as blasting rock in mines, building dams, and breaking up ice jams in rivers.

Kinds of Explosives

The three main types of explosives are mechanical, chemical, and nuclear. One kind of *mechanical* explosive is called *cardox*. Cardox consists of a sealed metal tube filled with liquid carbon dioxide and a means of heating the tube. Heat causes the liquid to become a gas that bursts the seal and expands rapidly. Cardox is a slow, low-powered explosive used in mines to split rock.

The two kinds of *chemical* explosives are the low and high explosives. A *low explosive,* or propellant, burns very rapidly after it is set afire. It explodes only when enclosed in a strong container. Otherwise, it simply burns in a flash. A large amount of gas results from burning a low explosive. This gas produces waves of very high pressure (shock waves) within a container, finally bursting it and making an explosion. *Gunpowder,* used in guns and fireworks, is a low explosive.

A *high explosive* is one in which

▲ The first guns were simple cannons that were built from wood and iron. They appeared in Europe in the 1300s after the arrival of gunpowder from China.

heat and gas are produced by a very fast chemical reaction. This reaction may be started by a shock caused by striking the explosive. Or it may be started by the shock of a small explosion in a device that is very sensitive to heat or impact, called a *detonator.* Blasting caps are detonators that explode and then cause dynamite to explode. Sometimes workers carelessly leave behind unused blasting caps when they finish their blasting. If you should ever find a blasting cap, do not touch it with anything because it can be very dangerous. Call a police officer or fire fighter to remove it safely.

High explosives generally expand faster and are more powerful than low explosives, so they are used where great, shattering force is needed, as in bombs and in explosives used to blast rock. Some important high explosives are trinitrotoluene, or TNT; picric acid; PETN; nitroglycerine; and RDX. High explosives cannot be used in guns. The suddenness of the explosion would blow the gun apart.

Nuclear explosives depend on the enormous temperature—millions of degrees—produced by either *nuclear fission* or *nuclear fusion.* The heat

The Chinese discovered how to mix saltpeter, sulfur, and charcoal together to make gunpowder. They first used it about A.D. 850. The mixture was packed in bamboo tubes, then stones and pieces of broken pottery were added as projectiles. From this came the idea of using gunpowder to fire a stone ball from a cannon.

▲ **Hiroshima, Japan, was reduced to a sea of rubble after the United States dropped an atomic bomb on the city in August 1945.**

▼ **Alfred Nobel, the Swedish inventor who developed several kinds of explosives, including dynamite.**

▼ ***Anxiety*, an eerie painting with a disturbing theme, by the Norwegian expressionist artist Edvard Munch.**

produced rapidly expands the surrounding air with extreme speed, giving it explosive force. Nuclear explosives are the most powerful. The atomic bomb explodes by fission, the hydrogen bomb by fusion.

The Chinese invented gunpowder, which they used in fireworks, in the A.D. 800s. The English scientist, Roger Bacon, wrote a formula for making gunpowder in the 1200s. It was first used in guns in the 1300s. Nitroglycerine was discovered in 1846, but it was so highly explosive that it was not used much. In 1867, the Swedish chemist, Alfred Nobel, discovered that nitroglycerine could be safely used if mixed with a type of earth called "kieselguhr." Nobel called the mixture dynamite, which was used for construction projects. The powerful high explosive TNT was invented in Germany and used in both world wars. During World War II, the atomic bomb was developed.

▶▶▶▶ **FIND OUT MORE** ◀◀◀◀
Fireworks; Gas; Guns and Rifles;
Nuclear Energy

🎭 EXPRESSIONISM

Have you ever gone to a favorite spot and found that it looked very different? Your favorite playground, for example, may normally seem like a

friendly, cheerful place. Go there alone early some Sunday morning, and it might feel lonely and uninviting. Your feelings "color" the way a place looks to you.

Feelings also color the way *expressionist* artists paint. They aim to show their feelings through their art. One of the first painters to do this was Vincent van Gogh (1853–1890). In his painting, *Portrait of Dr. Gachet* (pictured below), van Gogh captured both his own and the subject's sadness in the painting. The painting conveys not just the melancholy of Dr. Gachet, but also the general weariness of his time.

The other painting shown here is called *Anxiety,* which means "worry" or "concern." You could probably tell, even without knowing the title, that the people in this painting are unhappy. The artist Edvard Munch (1863–1944) chose dark, sad blues and violets to express his feel-

▼ ***Portrait of Dr. Gachet*, by Vincent van Gogh, has expressionistic qualities. Van Gogh captures both his own and his subject's feelings to create an uncomfortable, melancholy mood.**

ing of fear. See the big, sad eyes of the woman. Notice her pale greenish skin and her downturned mouth. The men have faces like skulls. The black, stiff clothes remind you of death and funerals.

The most disturbing fact is that you don't know why these people are all so worried. Munch doesn't give a clue. Has someone died? Is someone lost? Has a bomb struck? You will never know, but your thoughts about what has happened can go round and round as you look at the sad swirling background that completes the feeling of gloom.

Edvard Munch, one of the first and greatest expressionists, was born in Norway. He studied painting in France, but he spent most of his career in Germany. Munch's manner of expressing his feelings about a place or subject in colors and composition influenced other painters.

The expressionists in the early 1900s felt strongly about poverty, suffering, and violence. They felt that, by painting these subjects, they were being honest because they were painting what they themselves observed or felt. In fact, some expressionists even said that an artist who painted a beautiful scene of a sunny day with all the people smiling was not telling the truth.

Some expressionists wanted to shock people, to end the tradition of painting everything prettier than real life. They succeeded, for many people were repulsed by their work. For hundreds of years, artists had used caricatures (cartoons) to *exaggerate*, or enlarge, any unusual features a person had. Caricatures were usually meant to be funny, but the expressionists often exaggerated to make life seem sadder and uglier.

When Adolf Hitler and his National Socialists came to power in Germany, German expressionists were forbidden to paint. Many of these artists went to France, the United Kingdom, the United States, and other countries that allowed them greater artistic freedom. "Abstract" expressionism—where artists do not create recognizable figures—is a more recent variation of expressionism.

▶▶▶▶ **FIND OUT MORE** ◀◀◀◀
Impressionism; Modern Art; Van Gogh, Vincent

EXTRASENSORY PERCEPTION

Did you ever feel that you knew what a person was going to say just before he or she said it? You did not simply have a vague idea that person was going to say it, but you *knew* it. Perhaps you only made a very clever guess. Or perhaps you made use of extrasensory perception to read the person's mind.

▼ Dora Devant, blindfolded, demonstrates her ESP powers by reading the mind of her brother, David, as he "sends" his thoughts to her. This brother-and-sister mind-reading act was performed in the early 1900s.

If someone could be found who could accurately forecast catastrophes such as earthquakes, wars, airplane crashes, terrorist bombings, or even what the weather will be like at 10 A.M. next Tuesday, he or she would be of enormous value to everyone. It is because no one has yet been able to produce such forecasts that scientists believe that ESP is possible but unlikely.

Extra in this sense means "outside of." *Sensory* means "of the senses," which are sight, hearing, smell, touch, and taste. *Perception* means "being aware of." So extrasensory perception, often abbreviated ESP, is being aware of something by a means that is outside your senses.

Ever since ancient times, certain people have claimed extrasensory abilities. Some believed they knew the future, and they told fortunes. Others said they could read minds. A group of men met in London in 1882 and formed the Society for Psychical Research. They set out to apply scientific principles when investigating claims of extrasensory perception. Since then, other groups have tried to do the same thing. No one has ever

proved the claims, but research into ESP continues.

In 1930, Dr. J. B. Rhine of Duke University set up one of the first research programs into ESP. He and his coworkers did most of the original work into *telepathy*. Telepathy is the ability to read a person's mind or to send another person thoughts, without a word being said.

The ESP researchers used a deck of 25 cards with certain symbols, or signs, on them. Dr. Rhine claimed that many persons could tell what was on the cards even though these persons could not see them. Other researchers say that Dr. Rhine's experiments were not done scientifically, and therefore, his results did not prove that ESP exists.

▶▶▶▶ **FIND OUT MORE** ◀◀◀◀
Chance and Probability; Psychology

EYE

The eye is the organ of sight. Some animals have simple eyes, which can only "see" changes in brightness. Other animals have more highly developed eyes, which can see shapes, movement, and color. One of the most complex eyes is the human eye. Your eyes give you visual information about the world around you.

Parts of the Eye

The outside, transparent, protective layer of the eye is called the *cornea*. The *iris* lies behind it. This is a colored screen, which is blue, brown, gray, or a variation of these colors. The dark center is called the *pupil*. This dark circle opens up in the dark to let in more light. It closes in bright sunlight to reduce the amount of light entering the eye. This adjustment helps people see as much as possible under different light conditions.

The *lens* of the eye lies behind the pupil. It is a crystalline, transparent disk, thick in the middle and thin at

LEARN BY DOING

You can conduct your own experiments in ESP. First, try flipping a coin. Can you tell before the coin lands whether it will be "heads" or "tails"? If you flip the coin 100 times, the laws of chance say that you should have the right answer half the time, or on 50 tosses. If you answer right 60 or 70 times, perhaps you have had a little help from extrasensory perception.

Now try an experiment with a friend. Sit with your back to her. Have her flip the coin 100 times, and, each time it lands, have her think about the way it landed—"heads" or "tails." After each toss, she should write down how the coin landed, while you should try to "read" her thoughts before writing down how you think the coin landed. Compare notes after the last toss. Again, you should be right about half the time. How did you do? What do you think of extrasensory perception?

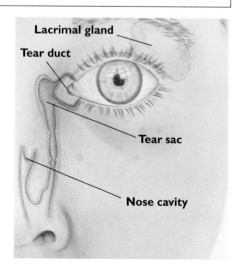

Lacrimal gland
Tear duct
Tear sac
Nose cavity

▶ Tiny passages connect the tear duct and tear sac of the eye to the nose cavity. This is why our noses often run when we cry.

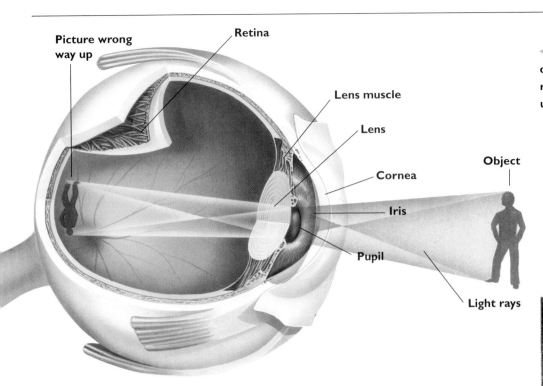

Picture wrong way up

Retina

Lens muscle

Lens

Cornea

Object

Iris

Pupil

Light rays

◀ **When you look at an object, the light rays reflected from it are focused upside down on your retina.**

the edges. It is about one-third of an inch (0.8 cm) in diameter. The central part of the lens is suspended by ligaments a little distance behind the pupil. Its function is to focus the light onto a screen that lines the back of the eyeball: the *retina*.

The retina consists of cells that are sensitive to light. It is made up of two types of light-sensitive cells, called rods and cones. Light strikes the retina, producing impulses that are transmitted by the nerves to the visual areas of the brain.

The cones perceive color and work best in good light. They respond to much stronger light than the rods. They enable us to see objects more precisely and in finer detail. The rods, on the other hand, are not sensitive to color, only black and white. They make it possible to see in dim light. When we work in a dim light, colors appear to fade and we tend to see things in tones of gray.

How the Eye Works

The eye works like a camera in many ways. Both focus light through a lens onto a screen to get a picture. The stop in the camera is like the pupil in the eye. You open up a camera stop to allow more light to reach the film

on a gray day. On a sunny day, you close the stop until only a tiny hole is left. This reduces the light striking the film when you trip the shutter.

When you use a complicated camera, you focus the picture you wish to throw on the film by moving the lens in and out. The human eye focuses in a similar way, through changes in the shape of the lens.

Muscles attached to the lens alter its shape. If you look at a distant object, the lens muscles are relaxed. But when you want to read fine print, the muscles of the lens make it thicker. This brings the near object into focus. You can find the near point of your vision by gradually bringing a pencil toward you and seeing the point at which it becomes blurred.

▲ **In dim light, the pupil opens wide. In bright light, it closes to a small point.**

▼ **Glasses can help correct near- and farsightedness.**

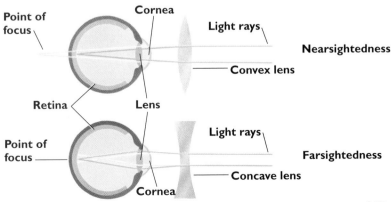

Point of focus

Cornea

Light rays

Nearsightedness

Convex lens

Retina

Lens

Point of focus

Light rays

Farsightedness

Concave lens

Cornea

Human

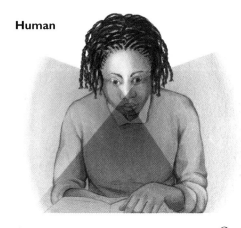

Owl

Hare

▲ Both humans and owls have large areas of *binocular vision,* which enables them to judge distances accurately. Hares, which have eyes at the sides of their heads, can see all the way around, but have a small area of binocular vision.

WHERE TO DISCOVER MORE

Hidden Worlds. Washington, D.C.: National Geographic Society, 1981.

Parker, Steve. *The Eye and Seeing.* New York: Watts, 1989.

One of the most familiar problems with being able to see is being *near-sighted.* This condition happens when the eyeball is very long or the cornea is too curved, so that the lens cannot focus on the retina for faraway objects. Other people have trouble seeing objects that are close. They are *farsighted.* The eyeball is too short or the cornea is not curved enough. This is often a problem of people over age 40. They need glasses for reading. Still another problem is *astigmatism,* caused by having an unevenly curved cornea. This causes blurred vision. Wearing glasses can correct these three problems.

Animal Eyes

The way an animal lives usually determines what kind of vision it has. Animals that fly or climb or eat other animals need better vision than those that live underground or eat plants. Insects have compound eyes, which are made up of cylindrical units called *ommatidia.* A tiny part of an object is seen on each cylinder and put together like a mosaic picture. The "eyes" of some invertebrates such as earthworms are simply special cells that are sensitive to light.

Some animals that have good vision and are active during the day in brightly lighted places can see different colors. Humans, most monkeys, the apes, birds, and some reptiles are capable of distinguishing colors.

▶▶▶▶ **FIND OUT MORE** ◀◀◀◀
Camera; Color Blindness; Dimension; Glasses; Sense Organ; Sight

▼ A horse-fly's eye is made up of hundreds of separate light-detecting units. Each one "sees" only a small part of a scene.

Close-up of fly's eye

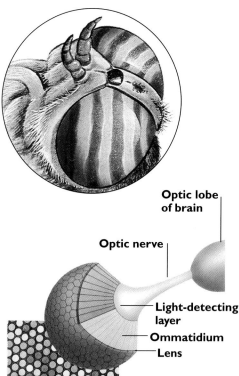

Optic lobe of brain

Optic nerve

Light-detecting layer

Ommatidium

Lens

LEARN BY DOING

You and a friend can see the pupil at work. Have your friend stand facing a bright light. He or she should cover both eyes with the hands. Count slowly to 25. Then remove the hands quickly. Watch the eyes carefully as you do this. Then change places and do the same thing. What did each of you see? What causes this?

FABLE

"Think twice before you act." "Laziness is its own punishment." Each of these sentences is the *moral* of a story. A moral is a bit of advice about how to live, or a truth about life. Morals are often taught by short stories called *fables*. Many have animal characters that behave like people. Some fables are poems.

"Think twice before you act" is the moral of a fable about two frogs. One frog wanted to jump into a well because the water looked so clear and inviting. But the other frog was afraid to jump. It was worried about how they would get out if the well dried up. Do you think this frog was wise?

"Laziness is its own punishment" is the moral of a fable about two lazy serving maids. A crowing rooster woke them early each morning. The maids killed the rooster so that they could sleep later. But from then on their mistress woke them up every morning. And she woke them even earlier than the rooster had.

Fables have been told for thousands of years. They were passed on by word of mouth from generation to generation. One of the great tellers of fables was Aesop. Legend says he was a slave who lived in Greece in the 500s B.C. His fables were not written down until about 200 years after his death. Another famous collection of fables was written in India some time before A.D. 500. It was written in the ancient language of Sanskrit and was called the *Panchatantra*.

A sly creature called Reynard the Fox was the clever hero of countless fables written in Europe during the

▲ An illustration from an old African fable that tells the story of a spider.

Middle Ages. One of the greatest fable-tellers of all time was Jean La Fontaine, a Frenchman. He published many books of fables in the 1600s. His fables are still famous all over the world. La Fontaine influenced many other writers. Hans Christian Andersen, the Danish author, used the fable idea in several of his fairy tales. The American writers George Ade, James Thurber, and William Saroyan have also written entertaining books of fables. Even some of Walt Disney's cartoon movies tell stories similar to fables.

▶▶▶▶ **FIND OUT MORE** ◀◀◀◀
Aesop; Andersen, Hans Christian;
La Fontaine, Jean

FABRE, J. HENRI (1823–1915)

Have you ever been amazed as you watched ants struggle to bring a huge piece of food back to their nest? Have you ever been fascinated by the engineering techniques that a spider must master to build its web? If so, you have shared a feeling of wonder with Henri Fabre, a great French *entomologist* (a scientist who

**DEVELOPMENT OF
THE LETTER F**

Y The Egyptian F
c. 3000 B.C.

Y The
Phoenician F
c. 1000 B.C.

F The Greek F
c. 600 B.C.

F The modern F
from the
Roman

FACSIMILE

Suppose you are an engineer who wants to show a client hundreds of miles away an important drawing of a new bridge. The client needs to see it right away. You can show the client a copy of the drawing within minutes by means of a *facsimile* or fax machine.

Fax is short for facsimile, which means an "exact copy." A tiny beam of light is passed over a black-and-white picture at the transmitting end. It is reflected into an electric "eye," which changes the light waves into electric current. The different tones of the original image produce fluctuations in the electric current. This current can then be sent over a telephone line or by radio.

One way to produce an instant copy at the receiving end is by passing the current through a chemically treated sheet of paper. The image appears as

▲ Henri Fabre was the first scientist to study living insects in the places where they live. He collected specimens in jars, and made careful notes and drawings of his observations.

studies insects). Fabre was one of the first persons ever to study living insects, rather than the dead, mounted specimens in a museum collection.

Jean-Henri Casimir Fabre came from a very poor family. He worked to pay for his studies at the University of Paris, and then became a teacher of chemistry and physics. He read a book on insects at the same time he started teaching. Fabre became so interested that he studied insects for the rest of his life.

In 1870, he was dismissed from his teaching post for admitting girls to his classes. For the next nine years, Fabre supported himself by writing books that explained science to children.

Fabre spent the last third of his life observing and writing about insects and spiders. He studied these creatures in the field and did experiments with them in his laboratory. His books on his work are still read by people interested in nature.

▶ A fax machine can transmit any marks on paper, from a sketchy drawing to typeset words. A scanner in the machine "reads" the paper line by line, detecting any dark patches and coding these as electrical signals. The signals travel to the receiving machine via the telephone network.

dots on the paper. Dark dots are made by a strong current, and light ones by a weak current. Another version of the fax machine produces a photographic copy by aiming a tiny beam of light at sensitized film.

▶▶▶▶ **FIND OUT MORE** ◀◀◀◀
Insect; Spider

FAIR

A fair is an event to which many people come to buy, sell, or show goods. The earliest fairs took place at times when large groups of people gathered to celebrate religious festivals. Farmers and craftsmen would bring

their goods and display them. Such fairs were held in ancient Greece, Rome, and China. Similar fairs were held throughout Europe during the Middle Ages.

Kings also gave certain cities special permission to have fairs. The region of Champagne in France became well known for its fairs, which featured goods such as furs from Russia, cloth from England, and spices from Asia. Other great fairs were held in Brussels in Belgium, Leipzig in Germany, and Stourbridge in England. A special fair just for showing horses was held each year in Nizhni Novgorod (now Gorki) in Russia. The Bartholomew Fair in London, England (first held in the 1100s), was held in honor of Saint Bartholomew, around his feast day on August 24. It was the first fair known for its plays and amusements, rather than for trade exhibits.

Fairs in the United States

County and state fairs are usually held once a year in the United States. In colonial days, fairs were simply for buying and selling. Farmers gathered to buy and sell seeds, livestock, and farming tools. In the 1800s, fairs began to feature demonstrations of better methods of raising crops and breeding livestock. Later, contests were added for the best fruits and vegetables, the finest handmade quilts, and the tastiest homemade jams, jellies, pies, and cakes. Prizes were also given for the best cows, pigs, and other farm animals. County and state fairs today often exhibit the latest farming equipment and provide amusement areas with rides, games, sideshows, races, and refreshment stands. Sometimes shows are performed featuring famous entertainers.

World's Fairs

Another kind of fair is the *exposition,* or world's fair. These fairs attract people from all over the world, and many nations take part in them. The exhibits demonstrate new ideas and achievements in industry, farming, science, and the arts. One of the first great world's fairs was held in London, England. Called the Great Exhibition, it was held in 1851 in the Crystal Palace, a magnificent building of glass and iron specially constructed for the fair. Many people thought the building was as wonder-

◄ Great fairs emerged along the main trading routes. This picture shows the fair at Lendit, France, in the 1400s.

▼ It was originally intended that the Crystal Palace, built for the 1851 Great Exhibition, would remain for only six months. However, when the Exhibition closed, a site at Sydenham, London, was found for it to be re-erected, though much altered and enlarged. It burned down in 1936, and was never rebuilt.

▲ Farmers exhibit their finest cattle at county fairs in the hope of winning a prize or ribbon.

The U.S. Bicentennial of July 4, 1976, celebrating the 200th anniversary of Independence, was a nationwide affair. There were fireworks, special musical events, fairs, and exhibits in towns and cities across the country. More than 6 million people watched the tall sailing ships from 31 nations parade up the Hudson River.

ful as the exhibits inside it. The United States sent 560 exhibits there, including Cyrus McCormick's grain reaper and displays of false teeth and artificial legs.

Other countries soon began to hold similar expositions. The Centennial Exposition, held in Philadelphia in 1876, celebrated the 100th anniversary of U.S. independence. Recent inventions of that time, such as the telephone and the typewriter, were shown. The Eiffel Tower in Paris, France, designed by Alexandre-Gustave Eiffel, was built for the Paris Exposition of 1889. Chicago was the site of the World's Columbian Exposition in 1893. It celebrated the 400th anniversary of the discovery of America. People who visited this exposition marveled at demonstrations of the latest developments in electricity. Many also took a thrilling ride on the first Ferris wheel, built especially for the occasion.

Some recent international expositions have been the 1975 World's Fair in Okinawa, Japan, centered on the theme of the world's ocean environment; the 1982 fair in Knoxville, Tennessee, which centered on the world's energy needs; the 1986 fair in Vancouver, Canada, centered on the theme of transportation; and the 1992 fair in Barcelona, Spain, which commemorated the 500th anniversary of Christopher Columbus' voyage to the New World.

World's fairs require long and careful planning. Proposals for the Chicago exposition of 1893 began in 1886. Construction began in 1890. And still the exposition opened a year late. The nations that participate in world's fairs also spend huge amounts of money to make their exhibits attractive and interesting to the public.

Most world's fair buildings and exhibits are destroyed when the exposition ends, but some remain, like the Eiffel Tower in Paris, France. The Palace of Fine Arts, San Francisco, from the 1915 exposition, was rebuilt in permanent materials. It was reopened in the late 1960s.

FAIRY TALE

Fairy tales often begin with the words "Once upon a time . . ." They take place in faraway, imaginary places where unusual events occur as if they were ordinary happenings. Long ago, when few people owned books, stories were passed down from generation to generation by word of mouth. Some of the tales were based on *folklore*, or the traditions of a group of people. Many of these stories, especially those for children, were written down and became the familiar fairy tales.

All fairy tales share certain features. Fairies, elves, leprechauns, trolls, brownies, pixies, and other creatures with magic powers are often important characters. But these imaginary creatures are not always included. Animals—both real and imaginary—may be in the story, too. Sometimes they can talk the way people do. Kings, queens, handsome princes, and beautiful princesses also take part.

Fairy tales may tell about an imaginary person's life and how the forces of good and evil challenge one another during the person's lifetime. For example, a wicked witch may

▲ The well-known story of "Goldilocks and the Three Bears" is an example of a fairy tale where the number three is important.

appeared at the banquet to say that the little princess would one day prick her finger on a spindle (part of a spinning wheel) and die. One of the good fairies changed the spell so that the princess would not die, but would only sleep for 100 years. She was awakened by a young prince who fought his way to her through thorn-covered bushes. The much-told tale of "Cinderella" and her glass slipper was another Perrault story, and so were "Bluebeard" and "Little Red Riding Hood."

The brothers Jakob and Wilhelm Grimm, who lived in Germany in the early 1800s, collected many folk-

▲ "Tom Thumb" is a fairy tale by the Grimm brothers about the adventures of a tiny man. Here he rides a horse far too big for him.

cast a spell that turns a little boy into a mushroom. Then, with the help of a kind fairy, the spell at last is broken. At the end of the tale, everything works out for the good characters, and the story often ends with "and they lived happily ever after."

In many stories, the number 3 is important. The main character may make three guesses, take three tries, or have three wishes. In other stories, there are three brothers or three sisters. Can you think of any other "threes" in fairy tales?

Some Famous Fairy Tales

One of the earliest collections of actual fairy tales appeared in 1697. A French man, Charles Perrault, published eight charming stories, called *Mother Goose's Fairy Tales*.

One of Perrault's stories was "The Sleeping Beauty," the story of a princess. All of the fairies in the kingdom were invited to a great banquet to present gifts to the baby princess. One aged fairy was forgotten, because she lived in a tower and had not been seen for many years. The old fairy was so angry that she

tales. Their book, *Grimm's Fairy Tales,* is famous all over the world. "Hansel and Gretel," "Snow White," and "Rumpelstiltskin" are among the stories they collected. These stories often told of violence and wicked deeds, though goodness usually triumphed.

Hans Christian Andersen of Denmark wrote many wonderful fairy

▲ The fairy tale of "The Pied Piper of Hamelin" is based on a poem written by Robert Browning, who based his poem on a legend. Here, the Pied Piper, playing a haunting tune, leads all the rats in the town of Hamelin (Germany), to the Weser River where they drown.

LEARN BY DOING

Find a book of fairy tales in the library. When you have finished reading the stories, choose the one you like the best. Act out the story with a group of your friends or members of your family. If you prefer, make up your own fairy tale to act out. Try to find a few costumes and props around the house. An old torn sheet might be just the right ball gown for a princess. Hats and crowns can be made with newspaper, crayons, and tape. What would you make fairy's wings from? An old large box can be cut up into shields or wands. Or leave the box whole and make it part of the scenery. A packing crate could be a castle or a dragon's cave. Scene changes can be shown by making large cardboard signs to hold up.

After all the actors have learned their lines, and the costumes and scenery are ready, it is time to present your play. Invite family members, neighbors, and friends to be your audience.

WHERE TO DISCOVER MORE

Cole, Joanna. *Best-loved Folktales of the World*. New York: Doubleday, 1983.
Grimm, Jacob. *The Complete Grimm's Fairy Tales*. New York: Pantheon Books, 1974.

Probably the best-known fairy tale is that written by the great playwright William Shakespeare. Called *A Midsummer Night's Dream*, it tells how the king and queen of the fairies became involved in the lives of mere mortals, largely because of the pranks of the mischievous fairy Puck.

tales. The amusing "Princess and the Pea," the sad "Little Match Girl," and the beloved "Little Mermaid" and "Ugly Duckling" are a few of his most famous stories.

Andrew Lang, a Scottish scholar, searched far and wide for fairy tales. He published his finds in a series of books called the Blue, Red, Green, and Yellow Fairy Books. Thomas Crofton Croker's book of Irish fairy tales is another excellent, well-known collection.

The Study of Fairy Tales

When the Grimm brothers published their collection of fairy tales, other writers began to think of the folktales of their own countries, and made up their own collections of tales. They discovered that many of the stories from different parts of the world are very much alike. Some scholars think that all folktales originally came from one source, perhaps the peoples of northern Europe. Other scholars feel that fairy tales began in India and were carried all over the world by merchants and wandering tribes.

▶▶▶▶ **FIND OUT MORE** ◀◀◀◀
Andersen, Hans Christian;
Arabian Nights; Children's Literature;
Elves and Fairies; Folklore;
Grimm Brothers;
Perrault, Charles

FALCONRY

Since ancient times people have trained falcons to hunt other birds and small animals. The sport of hunting with these birds is called hawking, or *falconry.*

Various types of falcons are used for hunting different types of quarry. All falcons belong to a group with the Latin name *Falco,* but, in addition, some members of Falco, such as the sparrow hawk, are called "hawks" in English. All hawks are powerful, fast fliers. They have strong legs and long toes tipped with sharp claws that grasp and hold the prey. Their sharp, hooked beaks help to kill the prey. Among the types of birds and animals hunted by falcons are wild ducks, pigeons, partridges, and geese. They also hunt rabbits and hares.

People who train and hunt with falcons are called *falconers.* The bird must be trained to sit quietly on the falconer's arm. Falconers wear a heavy leather glove called a *gauntlet* to protect their arms. The bird must be trained also to wear a hood that covers its eyes. The hood keeps it

▲ Hunting was a favorite pastime for wealthy people. Falcons were widely used in the hunt.

Northern harrier

Swainson's hawk

Red-tailed hawk

quiet. The falconer walks through fields until some prey is spotted, such as a small animal. Then the hood is pulled off the bird's head and it is released. The bird sights the prey, attacks it, and kills it. Some birds only grasp the prey and hold it tightly, but unharmed, until the falconer comes for it.

A hawk taken from the nest when young is called an *eyas*. A captured wild hawk is a *hawk of passage*. Hawks of passage are harder to train, but they are better fliers and hunters than eyas.

Falconry as a sport originated in China before 2000 B.C. and was practiced in Japan, India, and other Asian countries as early as 600 B.C. Many ancient Egyptian wall paintings show the sport of falconry. The Romans introduced the sport to Europe. Falconry later became extremely popular in England. In fact, during the Middle Ages, the type of hawk an English nobleman carried on his wrist indicated his rank!

Falconry is practiced in nearly every part of the world today, from North Africa to the Netherlands to the United States. Although it is still a popular sport, the popularity of falconry declined with the invention of firearms.

▶▶▶▶ **FIND OUT MORE** ◀◀◀◀
Birds of Prey; Sports

FALKLAND ISLANDS

This group of cool, windy, and damp islands form a British colony in the stormy South Atlantic Ocean, about 480 miles (770 km) northeast of the tip of South America. There are two large islands, East and West Falkland, and about 200 smaller ones. South Georgia Island and South Sandwich Island are dependencies of the Falklands. Nearly all of the Falkland islanders are of British descent. More than half of them live in Stanley, the capital. Sheep farming is the only industry, and wool is exported.

In 1690, a British captain, John Strong, became the first man to land on the islands. He named them for a British politician, Viscount Falkland. France made the first settlement here in 1764, followed by Britain in 1765. Five years later, Spain took over. But after nearby Argentina became independent from Spain, it claimed the islands, which Argentines call the *Islas Malvinas*. Britain reclaimed the islands in 1832, but Argentina never gave up its claim to own them. In 1914, the British won an important naval battle against Germany near the Falkland Islands.

On April 2, 1982, Argentine troops invaded the islands, but they were defeated by British forces in June. Britain then stationed troops on the islands to stop another invasion.

▲ Most hawks soar high above the ground looking for prey below. Their keen eyesight enables them to see prey such as rabbits nearly a mile away.

ARGENTINA

ATLANTIC OCEAN

FALKLAND ISLANDS

▼ Stanley, the capital of the Falkland Islands and chief town, is located on East Falkland Island.

975

Radioactive fallout is the cloud of radioactive particles that is thrown out by the explosion of a nuclear bomb or an accident at a nuclear power station. A nuclear explosion produces a fireball that rises at up to 300 miles per hour (500km/h). This causes a 200 miles-per-hour (300km/h) wind on the ground, which sucks dust and soil into the air. Radioactive particles from the explosion settle on this material, which falls back to Earth as fallout.

FALL

SEE AUTUMN

FALLOUT

Everyone has heard or read about the many advantages and disadvantages of nuclear energy. Among the advantages are inexpensive electric power, cures for cancer, and the absence of gases that pollute the air or contribute to the greenhouse effect. The disadvantages are the very dangerous by-products of nuclear reactions. The by-product that sometimes escapes from poorly controlled nuclear reactions is called *fallout*.

Scientists first thought that radioactive fallout came only from nuclear explosions from atomic bombs. However, they now realize that all nuclear reactions produce some type of fallout, which stays radioactive and harmful for a long time. In 1986, fallout from the damaged Chernobyl nuclear power station in the Ukraine was carried across Europe.

Substances that release energy by themselves are called *radioactive*. If this energy is strong enough, it becomes dangerous to life. All nuclear reactions produce radioac-

tivity, also called fallout, which, if released, can be carried long distances by wind or water. Living things exposed to this fallout may become sick or die.

▶ ▶ ▶ ▶ **FIND OUT MORE** ◀ ◀ ◀ ◀
Atom; Nuclear Energy; Radioactivity

FAMINE

Sometimes an area of a country, or even the whole country, does not have enough food to feed the people who live there. People go hungry and many even starve to death. This situation is called a *famine*. Many of the developing countries of Africa and Asia are subject to famine.

There are many causes of famine. Many countries have rapidly increasing populations and are able to grow enough food only for their needs when there is enough rain. When there is a drought, the crops fail, and famine results. The countries affected

▼ Fallout can be local, or it can travel in the wind before it is brought down in rain, snow, or fog many hundreds of miles from its source.

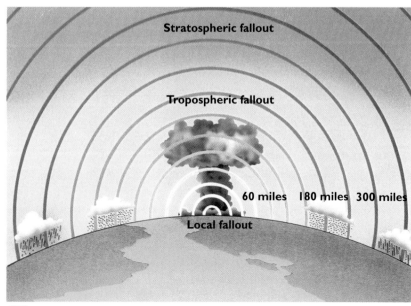

Stratospheric fallout

Tropospheric fallout

60 miles 180 miles 300 miles

Local fallout

▲ To aid famine areas, scientists have improved a species of rice, so that it does not droop and rot before harvesting.

may be too poor to buy food from other countries. The transport systems are bad, so food cannot be carried easily to places where it is desperately needed.

People of Africa have suffered from the effects of famine in recent years. A drought that began in 1983 lasted to 1985 and brought famine to 27 African countries. In the early 1990s, famine killed more than 300,000 people in Somalia. The United Nations sent troops to that country in 1992 in an effort to get food and medical supplies to the starving people.

Today, efforts are continuing to bring relief to similarly afflicted countries. Charitable organizations in western countries regularly send food and medical aid to these countries. A rock concert called "Live Aid," organized by singer Bob Geldof, raised more than $100 million to help feed the starving. But despite the efforts of many people, famine remains a serious problem in many parts of the world.

FARADAY, MICHAEL (1791–1867)

Michael Faraday is famous for his work in chemistry and physics. He was born in London, England. His family was too poor to keep him in school, so he started working for a bookseller at age 13. He read the books he handled every day, and he attended science lectures at night. Before long, he became a laboratory assistant to Sir Humphry Davy, a famous scientist of that time. Faraday learned much from his teacher.

Faraday's most important discovery was that electricity can be produced by magnetism in motion. The invention of electric motors and generators was made possible by this discovery. The basic laws of *electromagnetism*, *electrochemistry* (the studies of electricity and chemistry combined), and *electrometallurgy*

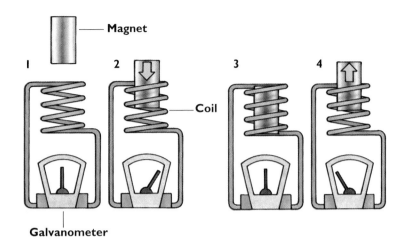

Magnet

Coil

Galvanometer

(using electricity to obtain metals) were set forth by Faraday.

His experiments led him to the idea that all space is "filled" with lines of force—gravitational, magnetic, electric, and thermal (heat). Other physicists developed Faraday's ideas, making possible the theories of Einstein and a revolution in physics.

The farad, a unit of electrical measurement, is named for Faraday. And the two basic laws of *electrolysis* (causing chemical changes through the use of an electric current) are known as Faraday's Laws.

▶▶▶▶ **FIND OUT MORE** ◀◀◀◀
Chemistry; Electricity; Electric Power; Electrolysis; Electromagnet; Element; Physics

FARM MACHINERY

Farmers once had few tools to help them in their jobs, and they had to work hard to grow enough food for their families. But many kinds of farm machinery have been invented to make their work easier. These inventions have made it possible for farmers to feed many people, by growing vast fields of crops or raising huge herds of livestock.

The *plow* is one of the farmer's oldest pieces of machinery. It digs up the earth before the seeds are planted. The cast-iron plow, patented by Charles Newbold in 1797, did not

▲ Electricity can be produced by magnetism in motion. No current flows when the magnet is stationary outside or inside the coil.

▲ Michael Faraday, the British scientist who discovered the principle of electromagnetic induction in 1831.

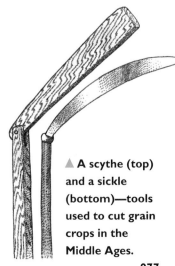

▲ A scythe (top) and a sickle (bottom)—tools used to cut grain crops in the Middle Ages.

977

wear out like earlier plows made of soft metals. Today a plow with four or more blades is hitched to a *tractor*, the farmer's most useful machine. The farmer drives the tractor through the field, and the plow is dragged behind it. A tractor-pulled plow can dig a wide, long strip of soil in a very short time.

When the plowing is finished, the soil is rough. Other machines, called *harrows*, are hauled by the tractor to smooth out the dirt. After the harrowing, seeds are planted by an *automatic planter*. This machine, also pulled by the tractor, has several containers filled with seed. It also has containers carrying dry or liquid fertilizer. As the machine moves, it drops the seed and fertilizer together into rows. The seeds are covered, and the planting is completed.

As the crop grows, it needs care. Weeds must be removed, and the soil must be kept soft. A machine called a *cultivator* does this job. A farmer may use other machines during the growing season. These include sprayers for insecticides, fertilizer distributors, and ditchdiggers.

Crops used to be harvested by hand. The first grain-harvesting machine used in the United States was invented by Cyrus McCormick in 1831. It was called a *reaper* and was pulled by a horse. Today, farmers use different machines to do this job. One is a *combine*, which combines several harvesting operations. It harvests wheat, oats, and other grains. Part of the combine, the *thresher*, removes the grain from the straw. It separates and cleans the grain to be stored. If the crop is hay, the farmer may use an automatic *baler*. This machine picks up hay that has been cut, and gathers it into big square, round, or oblong bales, tied with heavy cord. If the crop is corn, a *corn picker* is used to pick the ears from the plants.

A farmer usually hires a team of workers who own combines to harvest the crops. Combine owners start their work in the midsummer by harvesting the winter wheat in the south-central United States. They move northward, all the way to Canada, to harvest the spring wheat and other grains that ripen later in the summer and early fall.

Many other machines also help the farmer do work more quickly. Farmers who raise animals also use machinery. For example, poultry farmers may feed their turkeys automatically. They press a button on a control panel to mix and grind the corn and other foods. Compressed air blows the feed through pipes into different feeding troughs where the turkeys eat. And the dairy farmer uses electric machines for milking cows.

▶ ▶ ▶ ▶ **FIND OUT MORE** ◀ ◀ ◀ ◀
Cattle; Cotton; Dairy Farming; Fruit; Grain; McCormick, Cyrus; Rice; Tobacco; Truck Farming; Wheat; Whitney, Eli

▲The seed drill, invented by Jethro Tull, an English farmer, in 1701.

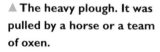
▲ The heavy plough. It was pulled by a horse or a team of oxen.

▼ Combine harvesters at work. This farm machine cuts and threshes grain or other crops in one operation.

FARRAGUT, DAVID (1801–1870)

"Damn the torpedoes! Full speed ahead!" exclaimed Captain David Glasgow Farragut during the Civil War battle of Mobile Bay. Farragut was the naval hero of the Union during the Civil War. To honor Farragut, Congress created the rank of admiral in 1866.

Farragut was born at Stony Point, near Knoxville, Tennessee. He was adopted by a naval officer after his mother died. He became a midshipman in the Navy when he was only nine years old. In those days, the U.S. Naval Academy did not exist, and naval officers were trained at sea. He took part in attacks on British ships during the War of 1812 and fought pirates in the West Indies during the 1820s. Farragut became a lieutenant in 1825. He was made a commander in 1841 and then a captain in 1855.

Although he was a Southerner, Farragut took the side of the North in the Civil War. He was given command of a Union (northern) fleet and was ordered to blockade Southern ports in the Gulf of Mexico. The blockade severely hindered the South from getting vital supplies and from sending its cotton to the markets of Europe. Farragut and his fleet captured New Orleans in April 1862, after a hard fought battle.

Farragut fought his greatest battle at Mobile Bay on August 5, 1864. The city of Mobile, Alabama, was protected by gunboats, forts, and underwater mines called "torpedoes." Farragut led his fleet into the bay. An officer warned him about the torpedoes. It was then that he gave the order that has become so well known. A fierce battle took place. Farragut and his ships won. The city of Mobile surrendered a few days later.

▶ ▶ ▶ ▶ **FIND OUT MORE** ◀ ◀ ◀ ◀
Civil War; Navy

FASCISM

The word *fascism* comes from the Latin word "fasces," describing a bundle of rods that enclose an ax. The blade of the ax sticks up above the rods. A red cord holds the rods around the ax. The fasces was carried ahead of ancient Roman officials as a symbol of power. The rods represent the power of punishment. The ax stands for the power over life and death. This ancient symbol of power has been used in modern times to represent the power and control of the fascist state over its people.

In a fascist state, the people must be absolutely loyal to the country and its government. Individual people must sacrifice their personal needs and wishes for the "collective good," or the good of the entire society. The "state" is supreme.

A fascist state is usually controlled by one person (a dictator), who controls the only existing political party. The party members are a small group of people who believe themselves to be superior to all other people, and therefore entitled to control or destroy anyone whom they consider to be disloyal to them. They want everyone to share their ideas and to work hard for certain goals. Those people who do not support them or who even mildly disagree with them are severely punished. Fascists often blame their own failures on various groups of people.

▲ David Farragut, naval hero of the Union in the Civil War.

> A salamander is a small lizard that can dart about quickly to avoid danger. Farragut moved his ships so rapidly out of enemy fire during the Civil War that he earned the name "Old Salamander."

▼ The fascist dictator Benito Mussolini (left) ruled Italy from 1922 to 1943. The fascist Nazi dictator Adolf Hitler (right) ruled Germany from 1933 to 1945.

▲ The Jews were persecuted by Hitler's fascist Nazis. They were forced to wear a yellow star (above) to show that they were Jewish.

▼ The *fasces* was a symbol of power in Rome. The wooden rods symbolized the power of punishment and the ax, power over life and death.

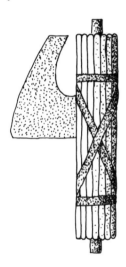

▲ General Francisco Franco, who led a fascist uprising against the Spanish Republican government. This rebellion led to civil war.

980

The fascists of Nazi Germany killed millions of Jews, Catholics, gypsies, and members of other minority groups that held different beliefs. These groups became the "scapegoats" for Germany's problems.

A fascist government has complete power over all the activities of its country, from what is printed in newspapers to what is taught in schools. Benito Mussolini and his political party had such control in Italy between 1922 and 1943. Germany was also a fascist state from 1933 to 1945, under the dictatorship of Adolf Hitler and his Nazi party. The German fascist government was *totalitarian*—it tried to control everything that the people did or thought. Anyone who did not obey was punished. At about the same time, the dictator General Francisco Franco created a fascist state in Spain after a bloody civil war that began in 1936. It was fought between the followers of Franco and those loyal to the Republic. Fascist governments have also existed in Asia, Africa, and Central and South America.

How do fascists manage to acquire such power? Usually the conditions in the country are bad. There is much unemployment and most people do not have enough money to buy the things they need. Sometimes the fascist party starts a campaign of written articles and speeches criticizing the existing government and telling the people that they are a superior nation and deserve better things. The fascists promise a glorious future for their nation. Many of the people believe them and, desiring a better life than their existing one, they often give fascists power by voting for them!

Once they are in control, the fascists try to make the people think that they have a part in the government by holding elections and political meetings. But the elections and meetings are controlled, and the people have no real control over national affairs. Fascist governments may

attempt to gain more land for their "superior" citizens to settle in—even if they must go to war to do this. Germany's desire for more *Lebensraum* ("living space") was one of the major causes of World War II.

▶ ▶ ▶ ▶ **FIND OUT MORE** ◀ ◀ ◀ ◀
Dictator; German History; Government; Hitler, Adolf; Italian History; Mussolini, Benito; Spanish History; World War II

FASHION

When many people start dressing a certain way, or buying a certain article of furniture or decoration, it has become a fashion. Changes in clothing fashions are usually the most obvious. People used to think that the custom of clothing the body began because of *modesty* (wanting to hide the body). But now it is thought that the main reason for the first clothing—aside from protection from weather—was to make oneself more attractive. This desire to look good may have determined most of the changes in fashion.

Clothing in ancient Egypt, Greece, and Rome was extremely simple. Egyptians wore little clothing, because of the hot climate. The clothing they did wear was of cotton or linen, the coolest materials. Both men and women, as is true in most hot climates, wore skirted instead of trousered clothing, either short or long. Their jewelry, however, was elaborate and was worn on all suitable parts of the body.

The early Greeks wore clothing made of materials with designs woven into them. But, when Athens became the dominant city-state of Greece, everyone started using the plain white material worn by Athenians. Fashions have very often been set in this way by countries that led or conquered other countries.

Greeks and Romans draped or

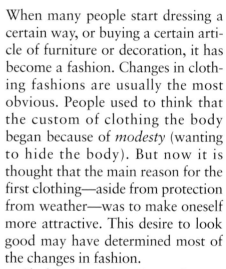

wrapped cloth around the body rather than cutting and fitting it. The common Roman garment for male citizens was the *toga*, a cloth wound around the body and covering one shoulder. The border or pattern on it indicated rank or office. Women wore a long, flowing dress, the *stola*. Under the outer garments both men and women wore *tunics* (loose garments with or without sleeves). The clothing of men and women did not differ greatly in appearance.

Early medieval Europeans continued to wear unfitted clothing, chiefly one or two tunics and cloaks. Up through the 1400s, men and women also wore long cloth stockings rather like tights. Floor-length robes were worn by both men and women. The biggest fashion change of this period occurred in the mid-1400s, when people began wearing clothes fitted to the body. Coats and vests were first worn by men about 1660.

Women continued to wear robes until about the 1500s, when they started wearing full, tight-waisted skirts held out from the body by a set of whalebone hoops called a *farthingale*. After this period, European styles began changing faster. Fashion change often goes along with changes in the world. Explorers were visiting faraway lands during this period. Europeans were visiting each other's countries more often. More people were living in large towns. They had more money to spend, and they met large numbers of people, unlike people of earlier times who lived in small villages all their lives.

New fabrics, such as silk brought back by explorers from China, began to be used. The wealthy wore clothing of soft velvet and fancy brocade, two fabrics that can be made from silk.

Some styles were begun by important or influential people. One of these was King Louis XIV of France. He began wearing extremely fancy silks, laces, and high heels, and he made his court gentlemen do the same. With these, he made himself and the crown seem more important.

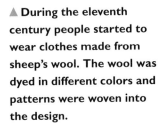

▲ During the eleventh century people started to wear clothes made from sheep's wool. The wool was dyed in different colors and patterns were woven into the design.

◄ A Viking man and woman in everyday clothes. These clothes were practical, rather than fashionable. They wore a lot of silver jewelry, which they sometimes cut up and used as money.

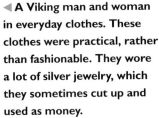

◄ This man and woman are wearing clothes that were fashionable at court in Europe around 1570. The men usually wore plainer colors than the women, but their doublets were often encrusted with jewels. Most rich women wore luxury fabrics such as velvet, brocade, silk, and lace.

◄ Over the past 200 years, everyday American fashions for men and women have become much simpler and more comfortable.

▼ Western fashion spread to Japan in the late 1800s. Below, a group of Japanese men and women in Western dress play musical instruments from the West.

Clothing was a symbol of power and grandeur that everyone could see.

Popular writers influenced fashion changes even before the days of swift mass communication. The French philosopher Jean-Jacques Rousseau wrote about the goodness of simple country life. Queen Marie Antoinette of France began to wear simple cotton gowns after reading Rousseau's novels and essays.

Certain countries have gained popularity in the eyes of others and thus influenced fashion. Empress Cather-

ine the Great of Russia visited France and returned home, telling of her admiration for French life and culture. The Russian upper classes then adopted French clothing, as well as the French language.

Clothing fashions have often been a way of expressing political views or even a whole way of looking at life. The plain, unchanging dress of English Puritans (some of the first European immigrants to America), the American Quakers, and some of the stricter Amish groups of Pennsylvania showed their belief that clothes were unimportant as decoration, and that material goods were not very important to life.

Uncomfortable clothing, or clothing that makes it difficult to move around, can show that the wearers are rich enough to live lives of ease. Hoop skirts, which were worn from the 1600s through much of the 1800s, were an example of this.

In the 1800s, men's clothing, at least, became more comfortable. Instead of knee-length, tight breeches and knee-high stockings, men began wearing long trousers allowing for more movement. The "lounge suit," much like today's business suit, began to be worn. This suit, and the more formal tailcoat, were adapted from sporting clothes, rather than from court dress—as formal wear had been previously.

Women's clothes continued to be stiff, full-skirted, tight-waisted, and overdecorated through most of the 1800s and early 1900s. The one exception was when Napoleon was Emperor of France and encouraged "Empire" styles like those of Greece and Rome. The "empire" waistline (above the natural waist) and loose, straight dresses were popular then.

Corsets were worn under the stiff bodices of women's dresses. They were often fastened so tightly that women fainted—but if a woman wanted to be fashionable she had to put up with an artificially tiny waistline.

Clothing for women became more loose and comfortable during and after World War I (1914–1918). The 1920s saw a complete change in female clothing. Corsets were no longer worn, and hemlines went up. This change took place after a great change in attitude toward women. Part of it was caused by women starting to work outside the home. They had to have greater ease of movement in their clothing.

Another big change in fashion in the 1900s was the adoption of more

▼ These girls are all wearing the full, calf-length skirt, and well-defined waistlines fashionable during the 1950s.

fashionable clothes by a larger group of people. Mass production of clothing made it possible for people to buy cheaper clothes that were stylish. In earlier times there was a huge division between the wealthy, whose styles changed with the season, and the poor or working people, who wore the same style year after year.

Today, many people travel, and television and newspapers go all over the world. Fashionable clothing styles have spread to countries where, formerly, an unchanging national costume was worn. People today wear extremely comfortable and informal clothing, even in places where people would once have worn stiff, formal dress. As with other fashions, these have followed from new ideas about the roles of men and women, and from the more informal ways people today speak, behave, and live.

▶ ▶ ▶ ▶ **FIND OUT MORE** ◀ ◀ ◀ ◀
Clothing; Feather; Hat; Jewelry; Knitting; Lace; Sewing; Shoes

◀ Two "flappers" and a friend in fashions popular in the 1920s. A flapper was a young woman who flaunted her unconventional dress style and behavior.

▲ Today's everyday fashions are informal and comfortable to wear. Children can run around and play in them easily, and adults can go about their daily activities in these clothes.

FATES

Three goddesses in ancient Greek and Roman myths were called the Fates. They were three sisters, daughters of Night, who were in charge of human life. The Greeks called them the *Moirai*. Clotho spun the thread

The British North America Act of 1867 created a Dominion of Canada made up of four provinces. These were Quebec (formerly Lower Canada), Ontario (formerly Upper Canada), Nova Scotia, and New Brunswick. A parliamentary system of government was also adopted.

of life; Lachesis measured its length (chance); and Atropos cut it with her shears (death). The collective Roman name for the Fates was *Parcae*, and their individual names were Nona, Decuma, and Morta.

Human beings did not want to die, and, according to the myths, they begged the Fates to stop spinning and cutting. They gave the Fates rich gifts and pleaded with them for longer life. But the stern Fates worked on, never heeding. There were Fates in many other mythologies as well, including the Norse, the Indian, and the German mythologies.

▶▶▶▶ **FIND OUT MORE** ◀◀◀◀

Gods and Goddesses; Mythology

FATHERS OF CONFEDERATION

Most of the British colonies in North America revolted against England in 1775 and formed the United States. But to the north, six British colonies still remained. They were Lower Canada (now Quebec), Upper Canada (now Ontario), New Brunswick, Nova Scotia, Prince Edward Island, and Newfoundland. The Fathers of Confederation were 33 delegates from these colonies who met at Quebec in 1864 to plan the creation of a united and independent country. They adopted a set of resolutions that led to the creation of the Dominion of Canada on July 1, 1867. Some of the delegates were in favor of calling the new nation the "Kingdom of Canada," but the name "Dominion" was finally chosen. All of the colonies, except Prince Edward Island and Newfoundland, joined the confederation.

The most colorful and vigorous father of the confederation was Sir John A. Macdonald (1815–1891), who became Canada's first prime minister. He encouraged western settlement and supported trade with Great Britain.

Macdonald's closest friend was George Cartier (1814–1873), a

FATHERS OF CONFEDERATION

Name	Region	Name	Region
Adams G. Archibald	Nova Scotia	Hector-Louis Langevin	Lower Canada
George Brown	Upper Canada	Jonathan McCully	Nova Scotia
Alexander Campbell	Upper Canada	Andrew A. Macdonald	Prince Edward Island
Frederick Bowker T. Carter	Newfoundland	John A. Macdonald	Upper Canada
George Etienne Cartier	Lower Canada	William McDougall	Upper Canada
Edward B. Chandler	New Brunswick	T. D'Arcy McGee	Lower Canada
Jean-Charles Chapais	Lower Canada	Peter Mitchell	New Brunswick
James Cockburn	Upper Canada	Oliver Mowat	Upper Canada
George Coles	Prince Edward Island	Edward Palmer	Prince Edward Island
Robert B. Dickey	Nova Scotia	William H. Pope	Prince Edward Island
Charles Fisher	New Brunswick	John W. Ritchie*	Nova Scotia
Alexander T. Galt	Lower Canada	Ambrose Shea	Newfoundland
Col. John Hamilton Gray	Prince Edward Island	William H. Steeves	New Brunswick
John Hamilton Gray	New Brunswick	Etienne-Paschal Taché	Lower Canada
Thomas H. Haviland	Prince Edward Island	S. Leonard Tilley	New Brunswick
William A. Henry	Nova Scotia	Charles Tupper	Nova Scotia
William P. Howland*	Upper Canada	Edward Whelan	Prince Edward Island
John M. Johnson	New Brunswick	Robert D. Wilmot*	New Brunswick

Lower Canada is now Quebec. Upper Canada is now Ontario. * Not among original 33, but helped win British approval in 1866.

◄The agreements reached by the Fathers of Confederation were legally binding in Canada until the Constitution Act replaced them in 1982.

People living in cold countries need more fat in their diet than do people in warm countries. Eskimos (Inuit) eat a great quantity of fat to store up fat in their bodies. This fat keeps them warm. All fat not used to give the body energy is stored as body fat.

French Canadian. It was largely due to Cartier's efforts that the French-speaking people of Quebec agreed to join their English-speaking neighbors and form a single country.

The stormiest father of the confederation was George Brown (1818–1880), a journalist and politician born in Scotland. He lived for a while in New York but found Americans "too democratic." He moved to Toronto and set about forming the Liberal Party, the chief rival of Macdonald's Conservatives. The newspaper he founded, now called the *Globe and Mail,* is one of Canada's most important papers.

Other well-known Fathers of Confederation were Sir Charles Tupper (1821–1915), whose efforts brought Nova Scotia into the confederation, and Thomas D'Arcy McGee (1825–1868), whose speeches aroused Canada's spirit of independence. The Fathers of Confederation had many different ideas, but they shared one dream—to create a new North American country, Canada, that would stretch from coast to coast.

▶▶▶▶ **FIND OUT MORE** ◄◄◄◄
Canada; Macdonald, John A.;
Prime Minister

FATS AND OILS

Animals and plants may eat or absorb more food than they need to keep alive and provide energy for the things they do. Living things store most of the extra food in their bodies as fats and oils. These substances can be stored because they do not dissolve in water, which is part of all living cells. Plants usually store fats and oils in seeds. Animals store fats and oils in all the tissues of their bodies.

Both fats and oils are made of carbon, hydrogen, and oxygen, which form compounds called *glycerides.* The main difference between fats and oils is that fats are solids and oils are liquids. (The oil that comes from oil wells is different from the fats and oils that come from plants and animals.)

Fats and oils are reserve materials that a living thing can use from its own body when its food supply does not provide

▼ Cooking oil is made largely from vegetable oils. Products such as soap and candles can be made from cow's milk and palm oil.

Cod liver oil

Soybean oil

Cow's milk

Whale oil

Pig lard

Rapeseed oil

Sunflower seed oil

Peanut oil

Olive oil

Palm oil

985

Sources of oils and fats

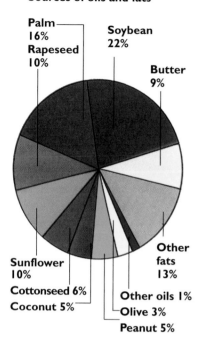

Palm 16%
Rapeseed 10%
Soybean 22%
Butter 9%
Other fats 13%
Other oils 1%
Olive 3%
Peanut 5%
Coconut 5%
Cottonseed 6%
Sunflower 10%

▲ Most of the world's production of fats and oils comes from plants.

▲ The legendary Faust is tempted to sell his soul to the Devil.

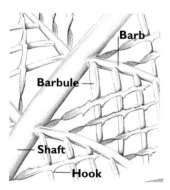

Barb
Barbule
Shaft
Hook

▲ A feather has a hollow shaft running down its middle, with many interlocking barbs and barbules coming off this.

enough fuel. A ground squirrel makes good use of fat. It builds up fatty reserves in its body during summer and autumn when food is plentiful. In winter, little food is available, so the squirrel hibernates, living off the stored fat.

Fats, proteins, and carbohydrates are the three main classes of foods. Fats (and oils) provide more than twice as much energy for the body to use as either proteins or carbohydrates. Most fats contain vitamins A and D. Vitamin D prevents the bone disease called rickets. Vitamin A is necessary for growth. Although we all need a certain amount of fats and oils in our diet, too much can be dangerous to our health. A diet with too much animal fat—found in butter, cream, and the fatty parts of meat—can cause the buildup of cholesterol in blood vessels. This can lead to heart disease.

Fats and oils are also important in industry. Plant fats are the basic ingredient of soap. Animal fat, called tallow, is used in candlemaking. Fats are also used in making drugs, paints, lubricants, waxes, and polishes, and many other products.

▶▶▶▶ **FIND OUT MORE** ◀◀◀◀
Chemistry; Hibernation; Nutrition; Petroleum

FAUST, JOHANN

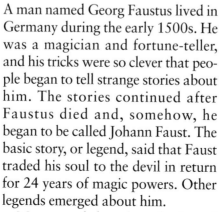

A man named Georg Faustus lived in Germany during the early 1500s. He was a magician and fortune-teller, and his tricks were so clever that people began to tell strange stories about him. The stories continued after Faustus died and, somehow, he began to be called Johann Faust. The basic story, or legend, said that Faust traded his soul to the devil in return for 24 years of magic powers. Other legends emerged about him.

Many people have been fascinated by his legend. Christopher Marlowe

(an English poet), Charles François Gounod and Louis-Hector Berlioz (two French composers), Johann Wolfgang von Goethe and Thomas Mann (two German authors), and many other writers and composers have used the legend of Johann Faust in their works.

FAX

SEE FACSIMILE

FEATHER

Have you ever heard someone say, "Like water off a duck's back"? What is so special about a duck's back? The backs of ducks (and all birds) are covered with feathers. Not only do these feathers keep birds warm and dry, but some feathers also help them swim! Some birds, including herons, have *powder down* feathers, whose ends disintegrate into a dry, waxy powder that spreads over the rest of the plumage. This waxy powder protects the feathers from water, causing the water to form "beads" and slide off, and adds to the bird's buoyancy when swimming! There are two principal kinds of feathers. *Contour* feathers cover the body, wings, and tail and are an important part of the bird's flight system. *Down* feathers are soft, silky feathers under the contour feathers. Down feathers provide warmth by trapping a layer of air.

People have used feathers in three principal ways. Before the invention of steel pens, most writing was done with *quill* pens. These are large contour feathers that have a sharpened quill (hard, hollow center) and a split point at the end.

Feathers have also been used to stuff pillows, quilts, and upholstery. With the invention of *synthetic* (artificial) stuffings, feather-stuffed objects are no longer as common.

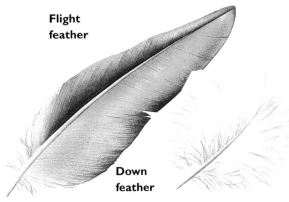

Flight
feather

Down
feather

▲ Flight feathers are the largest type of feather. Down feathers are closest to the bird's body and keep the bird warm.

But down feathers are still used as stuffing in expensive winter jackets, sleeping bags, and comforters.

Since prehistoric times, feathers have formed part of the decorative dress of people. Native Americans used eagle feathers in their headdress for identification. The position of the feather or the angle at which it was worn indicated the tribe of the wearer. In Europe and America, feathers have long been used by both men and women to decorate various parts of their clothing, including fans, hats, and capes. Women sometimes wore feathers in their hair.

The demand in the United States and in other countries for feathers to be used for ornamentation led to great slaughter of birds and the extinction or near-extinction of several species. Many societies and associations have been formed to promote the passage of laws which restrict the killing of birds for their feathers.

▶▶▶▶ **FIND OUT MORE** ◀◀◀◀
Audubon, John James; Bird;
Clothing; Pens and Pencils

FEBRUARY

The first Roman calendar had only ten months, and February was not among them. Numa Pompilius, a legendary king of Rome, is supposed to have added January as the eleventh

DATES OF SPECIAL EVENTS IN FEBRUARY

1	Supreme Court of the U.S. met for the first time (1790). Feast of Saint Brigid or Bridget, beloved saint of Ireland.
2	Treaty of Guadalupe Hidalgo signed. Mexico ceded New Mexico and California to the U.S. (1848). James Joyce, great Irish novelist, was born (1882). Groundhog Day. According to myth, if the sun is shining and the groundhog can see its shadow, there will be six more weeks of winter weather.
3	Felix Mendelssohn, German composer, was born (1809). Horace Greeley, American publisher, was born (1811).
4	Confederate States of America formed in Montgomery, Alabama (1861). Charles Lindbergh, American aviator, was born (1902).
6	Babe Ruth, great major league baseball player, was born (1895). President Ronald Reagan was born (1911).
7	Charles Dickens, English writer, was born (1812). Sinclair Lewis, American writer, was born (1885).
8	Jules Verne, French writer, was born (1828). Boy Scout Day, celebrated to commemorate the incorporation of the organization in the U.S. in 1910.
9	President William Henry Harrison was born (1773).
10	France ceded Canada to Great Britain (1763).
11	Thomas A. Edison, American inventor, was born (1847).
12	President Abraham Lincoln was born (1809). Charles Darwin, English scientist, was born (1809).
14	Valentine's Day, the Feast of Saint Valentine, when people send cards of greeting to people they like.
15	Galileo, Italian astronomer, was born (1564). Festival of San Isidro de Coronado in the town of that name in Costa Rica. Painted oxcarts parade through the streets.
18	Jefferson Davis became provisional president of the Confederate States (1861).
19	Nicolaus Copernicus, Polish astronomer, was born (1473). Edison patented his phonograph (1878).
20	John Glenn, first U.S. astronaut in orbit, orbited Earth three times (1962).
22	President George Washington was born (1732). Fréderic Chopin, Polish pianist and composer, was born (1810). Spain ceded Florida to the U.S. (1819). Robert Baden-Powell, founder of the Boy Scouts, was born (1857).
23	George Frederick Handel, English composer, was born in Germany (1633).
25	An income tax was set up by amendment of the Constitution—16th Amendment (1913).
26	Buffalo Bill was born (1846).
27	Hostilities were suspended in the Gulf War and President Bush announced "Kuwait is liberated; Iraq is defeated."
28	Vincent Massey became the first governor-general of Canada born in Canada (1952).

Amethyst

Violet

▲ The amethyst (top), is a semiprecious stone of a blue-violet or purple color. The violet (below), a blue-violet flower of early spring, is traditionally February's flower along with the primrose.

▶ Federal Bureau of Investigation agents wear a badge that features the American eagle and the scales and sword of justice.

month and February as the twelfth month. March was the first month. The name February comes from the Latin word *februare,* which means "to purify." It was the Romans' custom to purify themselves for the beginning of the new year. Later, Julius Caesar set up a new calendar. He moved the start of the year from March to January, and February became the second month. February has 28 days, except in *leap years,* when it has 29 days.

Americans celebrate many days in February. George Washington and Abraham Lincoln were both born in this month. Valentine's Day comes on the fourteenth, when old and young exchange Valentine cards or other tokens of affection. Groundhog Day is on the second of February. According to tradition, the groundhog (woodchuck) comes out of his burrow that day. If the sun is shining and the groundhog sees his shadow, he goes back to his burrow to sleep, and winter is supposed to last for six more weeks. If he sees no shadow, spring is supposed to come early. February 3 is Candlemas Day, celebrated by the Roman Catholic Church.

February's flowers are the violet and primrose. The purple amethyst is the birthstone of February.

▶▶▶▶ **FIND OUT MORE** ◀◀◀◀
Calendar; Holiday; Month

FEDERAL BUREAU OF INVESTIGATION

The Bureau of Investigation was founded in 1908 as a section of the United States Department of Justice. "Federal" was added to its name in 1935, officially making it the Federal Bureau of Investigation (FBI). The FBI *investigates* (gathers information about) violations of federal laws.

However, the FBI does not investigate *counterfeiting* (making imitation money) or violations of drug, tax, postal, or customs laws. Other government agencies are assigned to these crimes. Nor does the FBI take people to court. That is the job of the Attorney General or the police departments, to whom the FBI gives information.

From 1924 to 1972, J. Edgar Hoover was director of the FBI and helped it grow into one of the strongest law enforcement agencies in the world. In the mid-1970s, the bureau's abuses of power under Hoover were publicly criticized.

The FBI has headquarters in Washington, D.C., and offices in cities throughout the United States. It cooperates with police to solve many local crimes. Among the federal crimes the FBI investigates are civil rights' violations, aircraft hijackings, kidnappings (especially when they involve crossing state lines), espionage (spying), sabotage (destruction of property), interstate gambling and transportation of stolen goods, and attacks on or the killing of the U. S. President.

The FBI also gathers information about lawsuits involving the U. S. government. For reasons of national security, it keeps files on people and organizations important to the federal government. Because of these records, the FBI is often accused of "snooping"—investigating people's private lives unnecessarily. The FBI has the largest collection of fingerprints in the world. It also has a modern criminal laboratory, where scientists examine evidence sent from law enforcement offices across the nation. The FBI also cooperates with law enforcement agencies in other countries in matters such as the illegal traffic in drugs.

The special agents of the FBI are usually graduates of law or accounting schools. They undergo rigorous training at the FBI National Academy in Quantico, Virginia. Other law enforcement officers also attend the training course.

▶▶▶▶ **FIND OUT MORE** ◀◀◀◀

Detective; Fingerprint; United States Government; United States Government Agencies

FEET

SEE HANDS AND FEET

FENCING

Many European gentlemen of the 1700s were skilled in the art of fencing, or dueling, with swords. Until guns were invented, a combat with swords was a common way of settling an argument between two gentlemen, and men carried swords to defend themselves.

Modern fencing is different, because today the two opponents duel for sport and do not actually try to hurt each other. Some schools and colleges have fencing teams that compete against each other. Fencing is an international sport and is one of the sports in the Olympic Games.

Boys and girls who want to be good fencers must have good coordination between mind and muscles. That is, they must have good reflexes. Good fencers must be fast on their feet and must move quickly and accurately. Each fencer tries to outguess the opponent by figuring out the other fencer's next move.

The object of a fencing match is not to wound or kill. Instead, fencers try to touch their opponents with the tips of their weapons. At the same time, they try to evade and to knock aside their opponent's sword. That is known as a *parry*. A *riposte* is the quick forward thrust of the sword immediately after a fencer parries the oppo-

nent's weapon. *Touché* is the term used when a fencer touches an opponent with the sword.

Three types of swords are used in modern fencing. The most common is the *foil*, which is long, flexible, and tapered to a point. The point of the foil is not sharp, but is covered with a round pad so that it will do no harm. Another fencing weapon, the *épée*, is heavier and stiffer than the foil. The third type of sword used is the *sabre*, a wide, heavy blade, with which the fencer slashes at an opponent.

Fencers wear white canvas jackets or vests, well padded for protection.

▲ Today, fencing is thought of as an art form as well as a sport. It was first included in the Olympic Games in 1896.

Fencing was first practiced as a sport in Egypt as early as 1360 B.C. Its first governing body in Europe, however, was set up by England's King Henry VIII.

▼ Three fencing positions: 1. the salute, adopted at the beginning of a contest, 2. *en garde* (ready to begin), 3. the lunge (a sudden thrust). The three types of swords are shown with their target areas.

1
Foil
Target area

2
Épée
Target area

3
Sabre
Target area

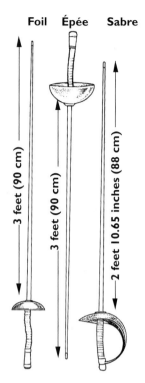

Foil   Épée   Sabre

3 feet (90 cm)

3 feet (90 cm)

2 feet 10.65 inches (88 cm)

▲ There are three types of fencing weapons: the foil (left), the épée (center), and the saber (right).

In 1854, the great French chemist, Louis Pasteur, decided to work on the fermentation of wine and beer. He showed that a living organism—yeast—caused the fermentation. To prevent wine going sour as it aged, Pasteur tried heating it to 120°F (49°C) to kill off the unwanted yeast cells. This technique became known as "pasteurization" and is still used to kill germs in milk.

▶ Enrico Fermi (1901–1954), a great Italian physicist, who produced the first nuclear chain reaction during World War II.

They wear metal helmets that have heavy wire-mesh face guards. In serious fencing competition, weapons are equipped with sensitive electric wires. When one fencer makes a "touch," a control panel lights up and a bell rings to indicate which fencer made the score. Opponents fence in an area 3 to 6 feet (1 to 2 m) wide and 40 to 60 feet (12 to 18 m) long. They are watched by a jury and by a director. The director announces a touch or a violation.

▶▶▶▶ **FIND OUT MORE** ◀◀◀◀
Duel; Sports; Swords and Knives

FERDINAND

SEE ISABELLA AND FERDINAND

FERMENTATION

Milk may become sour or turn to buttermilk. Apple juice may turn into hard cider, and then into vinegar. These changes are brought about by *fermentation*, a chemical change caused by many different kinds of bacteria, molds, and yeasts. All of these are plants so small that you need a microscope to see them. They secrete, or give off, chemicals called *enzymes*. An enzyme is a complicated chemical compound that speeds up the action of chemical changes—including fermentation—that take place in plants and animals or in materials that come from plants or animals. Enzymes play a very important part in digestion. They break down the food we eat into a form that can be absorbed and used as fuel by the body.

Enzymes in yeast, acting on the sugar in bread dough, form alcohol and carbon dioxide. The carbon dioxide gas fills the dough with bubbles, which make the dough rise. The alcohol vaporizes

when the bread is baked. Fermentation of fruits and grains produces ethyl alcohol for alcoholic beverages, such as beer. Medicines contain ethyl alcohol as a preservative.

In the kind of fermentation called *putrefaction*, bacteria cause dead plants and animals to *decompose* (break up slowly) into different chemical compounds. Most of these compounds mix with the soil and act as fertilizers. If it were not for decomposition, the whole surface of the Earth would long ago have been covered with dead plants and animals. Bacteria that carry out this form of fermentation are an important part of our ecosystem.

▶▶▶▶ **FIND OUT MORE** ◀◀◀◀
Alcoholic Beverage; Bacteria; Baking and Bakeries; Chemistry; Digestion; Enzyme; Food Web; Pasteur, Louis; Wines and Wine Making; Yeast

FERMI, ENRICO (1901–1954)

By leading the world into the Atomic Age, Enrico Fermi made advances and changes in the world situation as much as another Italian, Christopher Columbus, did 450 years before him. Fermi was a nuclear physicist who developed the basic principles of atomic, or nuclear, energy. He discovered that atoms can be split by bombarding them with very tiny particles called neutrons. This was especially important because neutrons can split uranium atoms, thus producing an enormous amount of energy. This energy is not only the destructive force in nuclear weapons, but also a source of power for many present-day and future inventions, such as the nuclear submarine.

Enrico Fermi was born in Rome, Italy. He received a doctorate degree in physics in 1922. Fermi taught physics at the University of Rome until 1938, when he

FERMI'S NUCLEAR REACTOR

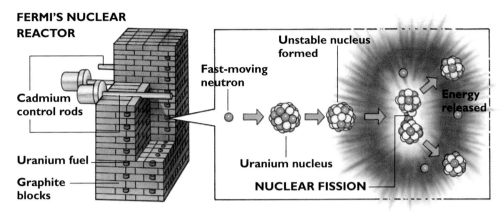

Cadmium control rods

Uranium fuel

Graphite blocks

Fast-moving neutron

Unstable nucleus formed

Uranium nucleus

NUCLEAR FISSION

Energy released

◄ Nuclear fission provides the energy for both nuclear power and atomic weapons. A neutron splits the nucleus of a uranium atom, giving off energy and releasing more neutrons. These go on to split another uranium nucleus, which gives off more heat and releases more neutrons in a chain reaction.

fled from the fascist government in Italy. He taught at Columbia University in New York City until 1942, and then at the University of Chicago. He won many awards, including the Nobel Prize in physics in 1938.

Fermi designed the first atomic pile (a nuclear reactor), a device for producing controlled nuclear energy. A squash court beneath an abandoned football stadium at the University of Chicago was selected as the place for building the atomic pile. It was completed in less than four months. On December 2, 1942, atomic energy was controlled for the first time. The success of this first atomic pile led to the development of the atom bomb and nuclear weapons.

▶▶▶▶ **FIND OUT MORE** ◄◄◄◄
Atom; Nuclear Energy; Radiation

FERN

If you walk in damp, shady places, you are almost certain to discover plants with large feathery leaves. These are ferns—green plants that have neither seeds nor flowers.

All you can see of most ferns are these lovely leaves, or *fronds*. Fern roots are underground, and so are the stems of most kinds of ferns. Some ferns have stems that "creep" along the surface of the ground or up the trunk of a tree. The leaves of many kinds of ferns are tightly coiled at first. The leaves slowly unroll as

they grow. These leaves are often called "fiddleheads." If you look at a violin, or fiddle, you will see how the leaves got their name.

Ferns grow almost everywhere on Earth, even in the bitter cold land north of the Arctic Circle. About 300 different kinds of ferns grow in North America. And about 10,000 different kinds grow throughout the world. Most types of fern appear in the tropics, especially in rain forests, where some *tree ferns* can grow to 65 feet (20 m) tall. Tree ferns look much like palm trees, with a crown of lacy fronds.

Some ferns have important uses. A drug used to treat people affected by a tapeworm comes from the *male fern*. Florists use the *wood fern* to make flower displays more beautiful. In the tropics, tree ferns are used for construction. Still other ferns are used as packing material. Some South Americans produce sugar from several kinds of ferns.

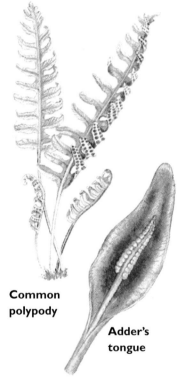

Common polypody

Adder's tongue

▲ The common polypody grows on rocks and walls in damp woods. The small adder's tongue looks more like a leaf than a fern. Its spores develop on the slender spike.

◄ The royal fern can be found in damp woods and other wet places. Although it is widely distributed in western Europe, the royal fern is rare in most regions.

FERRARO, GERALDINE

SEE VICE PRESIDENT

LEARN BY DOING

Ferns have a very complicated life cycle. To study this life cycle, go to a damp, shady place in early spring. The bank of a creek is a good spot. If you look carefully along the ground, you may find a few tiny heart-shaped ferns called fiddlehead or *prothallus* plants—each one may be smaller than a dime. Scoop up the plants with a little soil and put them in an open jar. Place the jar in a shady spot and keep the plants well watered. What happens? Keep a written record of how long each change takes. How long does it take for the fiddlehead to unwind? When the fronds are fully grown, can you find the spore cases on their undersides? New ferns will later grow from these spores.

Maidenhair fern

▼ **Ferns are found all over the world. They are flowerless plants that reproduce by scattering spores.**

Broad buckler fern

Hart's-tongue fern

Ferns are among the oldest of land plants. They first grew hundreds of millions of years ago. The decayed remains of these ancient plants gradually formed coal—one of the most important and useful plant products of all.

▶▶▶▶ **FIND OUT MORE** ◀◀◀◀
Coal; Horsetail; Plant

FERRARO, GERALDINE

SEE VICE PRESIDENT

FERTILIZATION

SEE REPRODUCTION

FERTILIZER

Growing plants use chemical elements that are found in soil. In time, the plants use up these substances. If more plants are to grow in the same soil, more of these elements must be added. Fertilizer puts the elements that plants need back into the soil.

Fertilizer is any material that makes soil richer in plant foods. For thousands of years, farmers fertilized their fields with horse manure, cow and sheep dung, crushed or ground bones, or chopped or whole dried fish. These fertilizers are still used in many parts of the world. In industrially developed countries, fertilizers are made by mixing chemicals.

Plants need large amounts of three elements—nitrogen, phosphorus, and potassium—to grow. Manufactured fertilizers contain quantities of these elements in a form that plants can use. Different portions of these elements are mixed in different fertilizers. Grass, for example, needs much nitrogen, while carrots need more potassium. Plants also need different amounts of calcium. Farmers and gardeners today can buy one fertilizer

▶ **To see the effects of fertilizer on plants, try growing some seedlings; one without fertilizer, one with too much, and one using the amount specified on the packet. Water all 3 regularly. After about a week, you will see the effects.**

that includes all of the elements that plants need. Or they can buy special fertilizers that provide only one or two of these substances. Users choose the fertilizer they need depending on the plants they are growing and the condition of the soil.

In recent years some people have argued that vegetables grown with the help of these fertilizers will contain chemicals that, over a period of time, could affect the health of those who eat them. Because of this, a number of growers have gone back to using organic—that is, natural—fertilizers.

▶ ▶ ▶ ▶ **FIND OUT MORE** ◀ ◀ ◀ ◀

Conservation; Ecology; Element; Plant; Soil

FEUDALISM

During the Middle Ages lands were ruled and held under a system called *feudalism*. This name comes from an old Latin word meaning "estate." A feud, which was usually called a *fief*, was a piece of land owned by one nobleman, who was called a *feudal lord*. He rented the land to another nobleman, who was called the *vassal* of the lord. A vassal swore to be loyal to his lord and promised to serve him. Whenever the lord asked, the vassal had to supply a certain number of *knights* to fight battles.

Most lords lived in fortified castles on large estates called *manors*. The common people—those not of noble birth—were called *serfs*. They lived in villages outside the lord's manor. Serfs had few rights. They had to stay on the land where they were born and work for the lord as shepherds

WHERE TO DISCOVER MORE

Anno, Mitsumasa. *Anno's Medieval World*. New York: Philomel Books, 1980.

Hunt, Jonathan. *Illuminations*. New York: Bradbury Press, 1989.

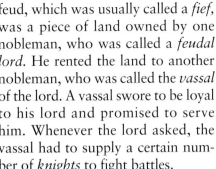
King

Pope

▼ Conflict between a king and the pope was common in the Middle Ages. The pope thought he had the right to choose the king and vice-versa. Everyone else, ranging from high clergy to laborers had to obey either the king or the pope.

High clergy

Nobility

Laborers

Soldiers

Monks

Farmers

The highest body temperature recorded so far is just under 116°F (46.5°C), when an American, Willie Jones, was admitted to a hospital in Georgia suffering from heat stroke!

▼ Natural fibers come from animals and plants. Wool and cotton are widely used natural fibers, while silk— spun by the silkworm —is the strongest. The stem of the flax plant contains the fibers used for making linen.

Cotton

Silk

Wool

Flax

or carvers or weavers. They were given small plots of land to farm, but they had to give the lord a part of all the crops they raised. In return, the lord protected them. In case of an invasion, the serfs could take shelter in the lord's castle.

Many different countries existed in the Middle Ages, but none had a strong central government. For example, one large area was called France. But it was not a single nation as it is today. It consisted of many fiefs. The king of France was no more powerful than many of the feudal lords. Each lord had authority over his own fief. Feudalism gradually died out with the growth of towns, craftsmen's guilds and trade, and unified central governments.

▶▶▶▶ **FIND OUT MORE** ◀◀◀◀
Castle; Fortifications; Knighthood;
Middle Ages

FEVER

When you are feeling sick, someone probably takes your temperature. If the thermometer reads higher than 98.6°F (37°C), you have a fever.

Fever is often a symptom of a disease or infection, which comes about when harmful bacteria or viruses invade the body and grow in large numbers. Because temperatures over 100°F (37.8°C) can kill some kinds of bacteria and viruses, many doctors believe that fever is one way the body fights against these invaders. Many diseases, such as scarlet fever, received their names because they bring on high fever.

A fever does not remain at a constant level. The difference between the highest and lowest temperatures may be as little as a few tenths of a

▶ A machine, called a jet assembly, "dry" spins a synthetic fiber made of cellulose acetate. You can see 28 filaments of the fiber in this photograph.

degree or as much as five degrees.

Whenever you have a fever, drink plenty of fluids and get enough rest so the body can build up its defenses. If the fever does not go away in 24 hours, you should see a doctor.

▶▶▶▶ **FIND OUT MORE** ◀◀◀◀
Bacteria; Childhood Diseases;
Disease; Virus

FIBER

Many of our clothes are made from fabric that is woven from thread or yarn. Each thread consists of many tiny strands called *fibers*. Traditionally these threads were made from natural fibers such as wool, cotton, or linen. Today, many of our clothes are made from man-made fibers. There are two kinds: One comes from a natural material such as cellulose; the other (called *synthetic*) is made by mixing different chemicals into plastics called *polymers*.

Synthetic fibers are made from certain plastics that can be drawn into long filaments. Nylon, which can be made from coal and other chemicals, is made by melting nylon chips and forcing the liquid through tiny holes. Synthetic fibers are stronger than nat-

ural fibers and do not crease as easily. But they do not "breathe" as easily and are difficult to dye. They are often mixed with natural fibers to make cloth. In recent years, super-tough fibers have been developed for use, for example, in the space program.

▶ ▶ ▶ ▶ **FIND OUT MORE** ◀ ◀ ◀ ◀
Plant Products; Synthetic; Textile

FIBER OPTICS

Imagine you are a doctor and you want to look inside a patient. Instead of doing a major operation, you could make a small cut and insert a fiber optic bundle. You could take photographs through the fiber optics.

An optical fiber is a flexible glass or plastic strand along which light can be sent. One fiber has a thickness of about 0.0005 to 0.006 inch (10 to 150 millionths of a meter). (A human hair is about 0.002 inch thick.) The fibers are usually used together in bundles. They are made so that very little light is lost, no matter how many bends or twists the fibers have to take. Laser light is often used.

Fiber optics are now being used instead of metal wires for telephone and similar systems. A single fiber can carry many thousands of telephone conversations at the same time.

▶ ▶ ▶ ▶ **FIND OUT MORE** ◀ ◀ ◀ ◀
Lasers and Masers

FIELD, CYRUS

SEE TELEGRAPH

FIELD HOCKEY

The origin of field hockey is unknown, but it is one of the oldest games played with a ball and sticks. For many centuries, field hockey was played by French men. It later spread to England, where it developed into a favorite men's sport in the mid-1800s. A group of English women began to play the game in 1887. After that, interest in field hockey spread to other countries. Girls and women in the United States began to play the sport in the early 1900s. Today, field hockey for women is a popular sport in the United States, especially among school and college girls. The U.S. Field Hockey Association supervises the sport and conducts regional and national tournaments each year. At the international level there are the World Cup and Olympic Games.

The hockey playing field is 90 to 100 yards (80 to 90 m) long and 50 or 60 yards (45 to 55 m) wide. A *goal*—a net held up by a wooden frame—stands at each end of the field. The goal is 12 feet (3.6 m) wide and 7 feet (2 m) high.

Field hockey players use curved *hockey sticks* about 3 feet (1 m) long. The players use the sticks to try to move the ball down the field and hit the ball into the other team's goal. The white field hockey ball is covered with leather or plastic and weighs about 5½ ounces (155 g). Scoring a goal counts one point in field hockey. A standard field hockey game consists of two 30-minute halves, also called playing periods.

There are 11 players on a field hockey team. Each team has five *forwards*, three *halfbacks*, two *full-*

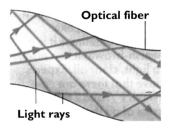

▲ **Optical fibers carry light. Any light that tries to escape from an optical fiber cable is reflected back into it.**

▲ **Field hockey players fight for control of the ball. This play is called a "bully."**

▼ **A diagram of a standard hockey field.**

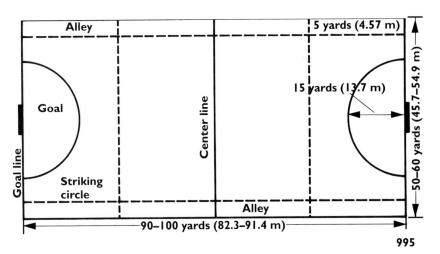

MILLARD FILLMORE THIRTEENTH PRESIDENT

JULY 10, 1850– MARCH 4, 1853

Born: January 7, 1800, Cayuga County, New York

Parents: Nathaniel and Phoebe Millard Fillmore

Education: Rural schools. Mostly self-educated

Religion: Unitarian

Occupation: Lawyer

Political Party: Whig

State represented: New York

Married: First: 1826, to Abigail Powers (1798–1853) Second: 1858, to Caroline Carmichael McIntosh (1813–1881)

Children: 1 son, 1 daughter (by first wife)

Died: March 8, 1874, Buffalo, New York

Buried: Buffalo, New York

backs, and a *goalkeeper.* Field hockey players wear padded shin guards and cleated shoes (shoes with grips). The goalkeeper wears heavy shoes and wide leg pads that extend up over the knee. Only the goalkeeper is allowed to kick the ball or to stop it with the foot. Body contact (such as blocking in football) is not allowed.

▶▶▶▶ **FIND OUT MORE** ◀◀◀◀
Sports

FIJI

SEE MELANESIA

FILLMORE, MILLARD (1800–1874)

In 1848, Millard Fillmore was elected Vice President of the United States. Only 18 months later, President Zachary Taylor died. Fillmore—who had won the Vice Presidential nomination by a single vote—was suddenly President of the United States.

Fillmore was born in a log cabin on a farm in Cayuga County, New York. He left school at 14 and became an *apprentice,* or helper, to a tailor. Young Millard was restless and unhappy, but his luck changed when a prominent judge in Buffalo, New York, gave him a part-time job. Millard did chores in the judge's office, and in his spare time he studied his employer's law books. He became a

lawyer in 1823 and served in the House of Representatives from 1833 to 1835 and from 1837 to 1843.

Fillmore became President at a time when the quarrels about slavery were beginning to divide the nation. Hoping to avoid civil war, he signed the Fugitive Slave Act. This law, passed by Congress in 1850, required that runaway slaves who had escaped to a free territory must be arrested and returned to their masters. This law aroused a storm of protest among antislavery groups in the North and was one of the reasons Fillmore was not President for a second term.

A few months before he left the White House, Fillmore took another step that later had important results. He sent a squadron of warships, under the command of Commodore Matthew C. Perry, to visit Japan. In a letter to the Japanese emperor, the President expressed the wish that the two nations should "live in friendship" and "trade with each other for the benefit of both."

By the time Commodore Perry was able to deliver the letter, Millard Fillmore was no longer in office. However, the treaty he had suggested was signed by the Japanese emperor in 1854. Few foreigners had been permitted to enter Japan before the treaty was signed. But soon Japan began to trade with the United States and with other western countries.

▶▶▶▶ **FIND OUT MORE** ◀◀◀◀
Civil War; Japan; Perry, Oliver; Taylor, Zachary

▶ **During his term as Vice President, Millard Fillmore chaired fierce Senate debates on the subject of slavery in the United States.**

FILM

SEE CAMERA; PHOTOGRAPHY

▶ Water is treated with chemicals and passed through a complicated filtration system before it is supplied to your home.

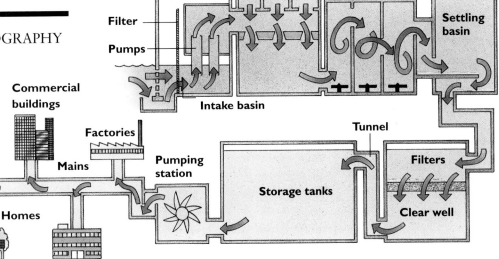

FILTER

When we are washing vegetables we often place them in a *colander* or strainer. The holes in a colander are small enough so that our peas or beans cannot go through them, but water and dirt can. The colander is a very simple form of filter.

A filter is anything that allows some things to go through but not others. We use them all the time. Air-conditioners have filters to prevent smoke and dust from entering a room. Water coolers have complicated filters to make the water you drink as pure as possible. We often make coffee using *filter paper*, which has tiny holes that allow water to seep through, leaving the coffee grains behind.

Other types of filters separate very different things. For example, if you were showing a school play you would probably use optical filters on some of the spotlights. These allow light of only one color to pass through, stopping all the other colors. *Magnetic filters* are sometimes used in industry. These remove stray grains of metal from, for example, machine oils. Automobile engines have filters for oil and air.

▶▶▶▶ **FIND OUT MORE** ◀◀◀◀
Automobile

LEARN BY DOING

Ask an adult to help you cut the top off a large plastic soda bottle. Turn the top upside-down and place it in the bottom half of the bottle. Put in a coffee filter paper and layers of wet sand and powdered charcoal. Pour muddy water through the filter. The water becomes cleaner as it drips through.

FINE ARTS

SEE ART; ART HISTORY

FINGERPRINT

Would you like to make a "picture" of a part of you that is different from that part of every other person who has ever lived or will live in the future? You can do this very easily, just by taking your fingerprints.

Sir Francis Galton, a British scientist, developed a system in the 1800s for comparing fingerprints. Impressions of a person's fingerprints can be taken by placing each fingertip on an ink pad and then pressing it on a card. A person's fingerprints are also left on any smooth surface he or she touches, even if they are not visible to the eye.

A system based on Sir Francis Galton's findings was later used for the identification of criminals by Sir

It is now possible to program a computer to hold details of the fingerprints of half a million people. In a few seconds the computer will match any of these with those of a suspect.

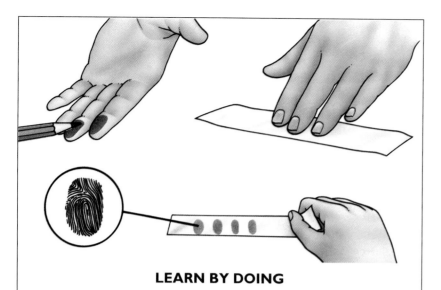

LEARN BY DOING

(1.) Sharpen a soft-leaded pencil and rub the side of the point across the balls of your fingers. Be careful not to prick yourself with the point of the pencil. The raised parts, or ridges, on the skin of your fingertips will be covered with gray powder. (2.) Press your finger tips against the sticky side of some transparent tape. (3.) Peel the tape away and stick it to a sheet of white paper. Examine your fingerprint marks carefully. They can never be made by any other person except you. Even identical twins have different fingerprints! Try taking the prints of several friends. What makes the fingerprints of each person different? Can you see any similarities between them?

▼ **Four of the most common kinds of fingerprint pattern are the arch, the whorl, the loop, and the composite.**

Edward Richard Henry, who became Commissioner of London's Metropolitan Police. The Federal Bureau of Investigation (FBI) in the United States began its fingerprint collection in 1924 to combat crime, based on Sir Henry's methods.

Any fingerprint impressions will show up if a fine powder is sprinkled over them. The impressions can be photographed. They will then be checked against the fingerprints on file at the FBI or any other large national law enforcement agency. To identify a set of fingerprints today, an expert will first classify the prints as one of four types—arches, loops, whorls, and composites. The prints will then be compared by computers with millions of others until they are finally matched with a name.

Fingerprints are not only used to identify criminals. The United States armed forces keeps a record of the fingerprints of all recruits. Aliens entering the country to live may be required to have their fingerprints taken. Many private businesses keep files of the fingerprints of their employees. Hospitals make palm and footprints of newborn babies. All these records help in the job of identifying people.

▶▶▶▶ **FIND OUT MORE** ◀◀◀◀
Detective; Federal Bureau of Investigation

FINLAND

Dark forests cover most of Finland. In summer, thousands of lakes sparkle among the trees. But Finland is in the extreme north of Europe, and the land is blanketed by snow for many months during the long, cold winter. A thick sheet of ice covers the lakes. Even the sea freezes along Finland's deeply indented coast, where there are many busy harbors.

The largest port is Helsinki, Finland's modern capital. Ships from distant countries unload cars, machinery, fruits, and vegetables at Helsinki's busy waterfront. The ships leave the port loaded with Finnish timber and paper. The timber comes from Finland's great forests. During winter, the Finns cut down pine, spruce, fir, and birch trees. Tractors push the logs to the shores of frozen lakes and rivers. When the ice melts in summer, the logs float along a network of lakes and streams to large sawmills. Finns call the forests "green gold" because timber is their main source of wealth. The soil in the interior of the country is too rocky for farming, so most farms are in the coastal areas in the south of Finland.

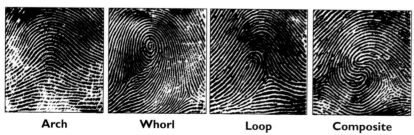

| Arch | Whorl | Loop | Composite |

Farmers have cut clearings into the forest to grow oats, barley, wheat, and potatoes.

Most Finns speak Finnish and Swedish, but Russian, German, and Lapp are spoken by some. All children between the ages of 7 and 15 must attend school. Nearly all Finns are Lutherans. But some are members of the Greek Orthodox Church, and others are Catholics or Jews. The Finnish people enjoy many sports. Skiing, ice hockey, swimming, and running are popular.

The Finns have made many contributions to the arts. Eliel Saarinen and his son, Eero, were important modern architects. Jean Sibelius was a world famous composer. Finnish artists have made many beautiful designs in pottery and glassware, as well as in other crafts.

Throughout their history, the Finns have fought bravely against their stronger neighbors, Sweden and Russia. Swedish Vikings raided the coasts of Finland a thousand years ago. By the 1200s, Swedish armies had conquered the whole country. The Swedes ruled Finland until 1809, when the country was conquered by Russia. When a Communist revolution broke out in Russia in 1917, the Finns declared independence. Russia attacked Finland again at the start of World War II. Finland was forced to give up some territory but has remained a free, democratic republic.

▶▶▶▶ **FIND OUT MORE** ◀◀◀◀
Europe; Lapland; Scandinavian Languages; World War II

FIORD

SEE SEACOAST

FIRE

Fire is the heat and light that come from burning materials. A material that burns is one that can combine quickly with the oxygen of the air. Not all materials can do this.

Most materials that burn are made up of chemical compounds containing large amounts of the elements carbon and hydrogen. Another name for burning is *combustion*.

An old proverb says, "Fire is a good servant and a bad master." Fire has been a servant from times long before history was written. Fire kept

FINLAND

Capital city
Helsinki
(987,000 people)

Area
130,129 square miles
(337,032 sq. km)

Population
4,971,000 people

Government
Republic

Natural resources
Lumber, copper, zinc, iron ore, silver

Export products
Paper, wood products, clothing, machinery

Unit of money
Markka

Official languages
Finnish and Swedish

Mt. Haltia
4,357 ft.
1,328 m.

LAPLAND

L. Inari
Ivalo
Muonio
Kolari
Rovaniemi
Tornio
Kemi
Oulu
Kajaani
L. Oulo
L. Pielinen
Kokkola
Vaasa
Seinajoki
Kuopio
Joensuu
Varkaus
Paijanne
L. Nasi
Jyvaskyla
Savonlinna
Mikkeli
Pori
Tampere
Saimaa
Rauma
Imatra
Hameenlinna
Lahti
Lappeenranta
Kouvola
Hyvinkaa
Aland Is.
Turku
Vantaa
Kotka
Maarianhamina
Espoo
Helsinki
BALTIC SEA
Gulf of Finland

GULF OF BOTHNIA

N W E S

0   100   200 Miles
0   100   200   300 Kilometers
© 1994 GeoSystems, an R.R. Donnelley & Sons Company

▲ **Reindeer are reared in the north of Finland (Lapland), either as working animals, or for their milk, skin, and meat.**

An early human makes fire by using a bow to spin the sharpened point of a stick into a piece of wood.

Stone-age people found they could make sparks by striking two flints together.

When a match is struck against a rough surface, friction makes the head of the match heat up and ignite.

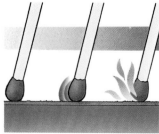

early people warm and protected them from animals. Fire provided light and cooked their food. There is no record of a human community that did not have fire. Human beings are the only animals that ever learned how to use fire. For thousands of years, people worshiped fire.

Fire keeps us warm and cooks our food. Fire also heats water to steam, which is used to run hundreds of different kinds of engines. Fire is used in thousands of industrial processes, such as making steel and separating metals from their ores. Fire from burning gasoline, oil, or jet fuel powers automobiles, boats, and airplanes. But fire is a terribly "bad master" when it gets out of control, destroying homes, other buildings, and even whole towns, as well as huge forests and prairies.

Three conditions must be met before the chemical reaction called fire can occur. 1. A substance that can burn—a fuel—must be present. Wood and gasoline make good fuel; stone and water do not. 2. The fuel must be heated until it reaches its *ignition temperature,* the temperature at which the fuel can easily combine with oxygen. Wood and gasoline do not ignite at room temperature. But the chemical called white phosphorus must be kept under water at normal temperatures, or it bursts into flame. The ignition temperature of paper is about 360°F (180° C), while wood ignites at about 500°F (260°C), depending on the kind of wood used. 3. A good supply of oxygen—usually from the air—must be available. Until matches were invented about 150 years ago, fires were started by borrowing burning wood or coal from another fire. If no fire was nearby, a pile of twigs or wood shavings could be set afire with

sparks produced by striking metal against flint, a hard stone.

▶▶▶▶ **FIND OUT MORE** ◀◀◀◀
Chemistry; Fire Fighting;
Fire Prevention; Forest Fire; Match

FIREARM

SEE GUNS AND RIFLES

FIRE DEPARTMENT

SEE FIRE FIGHTING

FIRE EXTINGUISHER

When a fire starts to burn out of control, a fire extinguisher may be used to put out the blaze. A fire can be put out in two ways—by preventing the oxygen in the air from reaching the burning material, or by cooling it below its *ignition temperature*—the temperature at which it burns.

The simplest fire extinguisher is water, which cools burning materials. One kind of fire extinguisher contains pressurized water. When the trigger on the tank is pulled, the nozzle forces out the water that is stored inside. The pressurized-water fire extinguisher is used in many schools today. But water must not be used on electrical or gasoline fires. It spreads burning gasoline over a larger area, and it *conducts* (carries) electricity, which may cause injuries.

Various kinds of fire extinguishers use different chemicals inside a metal tank. A *carbon dioxide* fire extinguisher contains compressed carbon dioxide gas. When it is released, the gas expands and cools, and this can lower the temperature of the burning material. More important, carbon dioxide does not burn and is heavier than air. It spreads over the burning

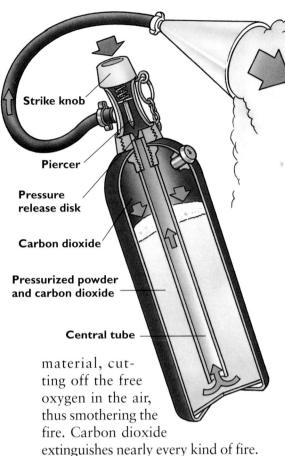

Strike knob

Piercer

Pressure release disk

Carbon dioxide

Pressurized powder and carbon dioxide

Central tube

LEARN BY DOING

You can do an experiment that shows how a carbon dioxide extinguisher works. Be sure to ask an adult to help you. Hold a long, lighted fireplace match inside a drinking glass. If you do not have any long matches, hold a short one with tweezers. The match will burn because the air in the glass contains oxygen. Now place two teaspoons of baking soda and 1/4 cup of vinegar in the glass. When the foaming stops, hold a lighted match inside the glass. What happens? How do you explain the change? The vinegar and soda produced carbon dioxide. This gas took the place of the air (oxygen) in the glass.

material, cutting off the free oxygen in the air, thus smothering the fire. Carbon dioxide extinguishes nearly every kind of fire.

For ordinary fires—not electric or gasoline fires—a *pressurized water* extinguisher is useful. It is simple to use. It has replaced the old soda-acid type, in which the reaction of soda and acid formed a gas that forced the liquid out.

Foam fire extinguishers spray foam made by adding detergents and other chemicals to water. The foam spreads over the burning material, cutting off the air from it. Foam extinguishers are good for gasoline fires, but not for electrical ones.

▶▶▶▶ FIND OUT MORE ◀◀◀◀
Fire; Fire Fighting

⚙ FIRE FIGHTING

Have you ever watched fire engines speed by on their way to a fire? The sirens scream, the bells clang, and there is a tremendous amount of excitement. Fires cause more than $7 billion worth of damage, kill about 6,000 persons, and injure

almost 30,000 others in the United States each year.

Every city and large town has a full-time fire department that tries to put out fires as quickly as possible. There are about 27,000 paid and volunteer fire departments in the United States. Smaller towns and villages may have volunteer fire departments. The persons who belong to a volunteer fire department are not paid to be fire fighters. They have other full-time jobs. But when the fire siren goes off at the firehouse, they drop whatever they are doing and get to their fire engines.

In colonial times, all the people of a town or village helped to put out a fire. People had to keep special fire buckets in their houses. Whenever there was a fire, all the people rushed to the burning house with their buckets. They formed two lines. One line of people passed buckets of water,

◀ A carbon dioxide-type extinguisher works when the strike knob is hit. This forces the piercer down, releasing the carbon dioxide gas. The gas settles over the fire, smothering it like a blanket.

▼ Steam-powered fire pumps pulled by teams of horses were an early kind of fire engine. They could shoot jets of water as high as the top of a flagpole.

**WHERE TO
DISCOVER MORE**

Marston, Hope Irvin. *Fire Trucks*. New York: Dodd, Mead, 1984.
Wolf, Bernard. *Firehouse*. New York: Morrow, 1983.

▼ **Fire fighters have to wear special protective clothing made of aluminum to fight particularly fierce fires. Without these special suits, the fire fighters would not be able to withstand the extreme temperatures or the flames of the fire.**

filled from a nearby well, toward the burning house. The water was thrown onto the fire. The other line of people then passed the empty buckets back to the well to be refilled.

These bucket brigades did not work very well, especially as taller and larger buildings were built. The cities in colonial America soon ordered hand-operated pumps mounted on four-wheeled wagons. These pump wagons were pulled to a fire by a group of people. Persons stood on each side of the wagon and operated the pump by working two long wooden bars up and down like a seesaw. The pump drew the water from a large wooden tub and threw a stream of water onto the burning building. However, it was still necessary for a bucket brigade to fill the tub with water.

As towns and cities grew larger, these crews of ordinary citizens were replaced by volunteer fire fighters who received special training. The first volunteer fire department was established in Philadelphia by Benjamin Franklin in 1736.

The invention of pumps that were operated by steam engines instead of by people was a great improvement in fighting fires. The first steam-operated fire pump was used in New York City in 1840. This pump could throw a stream of water as high as a flagpole. The steam-operated pumps were pulled by teams of horses.

Large cities also began installing special underground systems of water pipes, and outlets called *fire hydrants* to use in fighting fires. Pressure hydrants were first used in Rochester, New York, in 1874. Today, fire hydrants are located on every street of a city. When a fire engine arrives at the scene of a fire, the fire fighters connect the water hose directly to the nearest fire hydrant and get all the water they need.

The replacement of the horse-drawn steam engine by the gasoline-driven fire truck was the last big advance in fire fighting. Today, all fire trucks and all the equipment on the trucks are operated by gasoline or diesel engines.

Fire Equipment
The most important piece of equipment in any fire department is the pumper. The pumper is usually the

first fire truck to reach the scene of a fire. The pumper has a powerful pump that can spray from 750 to 1,500 gallons (2,800 to 5,700 liters) of water on a fire every minute. The pumper carries all the hose that is needed to fight the fire, usually about 1,800 feet (549 m). The pumper also carries ladders, axes, hooks, crowbars, and other equipment the fire fighters need to get at the source of a fire in a burning building.

A *ladder truck* is also sent to most fires. The ladder truck carries a long ladder that can be raised or lowered automatically. Modern ladder trucks have special platforms instead of ladders. These platforms rise up to 135 feet (23 m) high. They are used to rescue people from burning buildings, and they help carry hoses closer to the fire to put them out.

Putting Out a Fire

When fire fighters reach a burning building, they hook up their hoses to hydrants and rescue people trapped inside. They also break holes in the roof, and in the windows on the floor above the fire. They are "ventilating" the building—that is, they are letting out all the smoke and hot air trapped inside the building. If they did not let out all of the hot air and smoke, they could not get close enough to the fire to stop it.

The method used to put out a fire depends on what kind of material is burning. Water is used on burning wood, cloth, and paper. The water stops the fire by cooling whatever is burning. Fire fighters used to pour a solid stream of water on a fire. Then it was discovered that a spray of water would cool burning material even faster than a solid stream of water. Fire fighters now have special nozzles on the ends of their hoses that shoot out a thick spray of water that smothers the fire.

Fires in which a liquid such as gasoline or oil is burning must be smothered. Water would only spread

the burning liquid. Fire fighters use special chemical sprays or foams to smother such fires. The spray or foam stops the fire by preventing any oxygen from reaching the gasoline or oil. Chemicals that cannot conduct electricity are used to smother fires in electrical equipment or wiring. Since water conducts electricity, water must never be used on an electrical fire.

What to Do in Case of a Fire

Did you ever stop to think of what you would do if your house ever caught fire? If you know what to do in a fire, you may be able to escape without harm. Learn how to contact

▲ An airport fire engine sprays foam onto a burning airplane. The foam smothers the fire by preventing oxygen from reaching it.

▼ An airplane dumps chemicals on a forest fire in California's Sierra Nevada mountains. About 3 million acres of forest are destroyed by forest fires each year.

LEARN BY DOING

We can all help to prevent fires simply by being careful and by being aware of situations that could cause fires. Make a list of these dangerous situations that could cause fires. If any fire hazards exist in your home, help your family to get rid of them.

Big airports must have efficient fire-fighting services. The largest of all fire appliances are the crash tenders found at international airports. These powerful machines can produce 30,000 gallons (114,000 liters) of smothering foam in a matter of seconds. This is enough to cover a big jumbo jet completely.

▼ **Probably the worst fire of all time happened in London, England, in 1666. The fire started in a baker's shop and raged for four days. It spread quickly because of the narrow streets and wooden houses. These circumstances meant little could be done to prevent the fire from spreading. About four-fifths of the city was destroyed.**

the fire department. In many cities, *call boxes* connected directly to fire houses are located along the streets, or you can use the telephone to dial 911 for help.

Here are some important things to remember when a fire starts. Leave the building immediately. Close every door you pass through as you leave. This keeps the fire from spreading quickly. If you come to a closed door that feels hot, do not open the door. The fire may be blazing just inside the next room. If there is smoke inside a room or hallway, crawl through the smoky part on your hands and knees. The smoke is very poisonous and the best air will be close to the floor. If you live in an apartment house, use the fire escape or fire stairs to reach the outside. If your clothing is on fire, roll on the ground until the flames are smothered. As soon as you are out of danger, notify the fire department by pulling a fire alarm or by telephoning.

▶▶▶▶ **FIND OUT MORE** ◀◀◀◀
Fire; Fire Extinguisher; Fire Prevention; Forest Fire

FIRE PREVENTION

One day, a three-year-old girl picked up a box of matches in her home. She played with the matches for a while. Suddenly a few of them burst into flame, her dress caught fire, and she screamed. Her mother rushed in, grabbed a small rug, and smothered the flames. The girl was not badly burned, but she could have been.

This accident would not have happened if the little girl's parents had put the box of matches where she could not reach them. Many homes are destroyed by fire each year by just such careless behavior.

Hundreds of fires that have destroyed property and killed people could have been prevented by taking a few *precautions* (things done in advance to prevent dangerous situations). For example, people often leave newspapers and oil-soaked rags in a closed space, such as a closet or garage. When the papers become soaked with oil, they build up heat. The heat has no room to escape, so the papers and rags get hotter and hotter. Finally, they reach their ignition point, the temperature at which they will burn, and fire flares up. This is called *spontaneous combustion*.

Many substances are highly *flammable*. This means they can be easily set on fire and will burn rapidly before any attempt can be made to

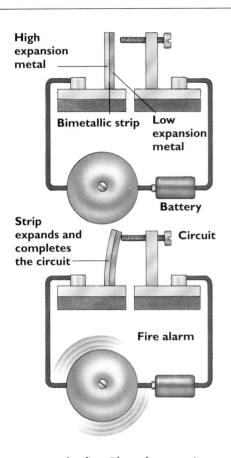

High expansion metal

Bimetallic strip

Low expansion metal

Battery

Strip expands and completes the circuit

Circuit

Fire alarm

put out the fire. If a substance is *nonflammable,* or fire resistant, it will not catch fire easily. If a fire touches a nonflammable substance, it will burn only the spot it touches—the fire will not spread.

Paint, grease, and other flammable substances should be kept in tightly closed metal containers. Electric wires should be replaced when they are worn, because they may make sparks. Worn wires on Christmas tree lights may set fire to the tree. Christmas tree decorations should be fireproof, and metal decorations should not touch the lights, for they can get very hot.

Sometimes people plug in too many electrical appliances at one time. This overloads the house wiring and can result in fire. Fires can also be caused by soot and dirt in chimneys, so chimneys should be kept clean. Fireplaces should have screens in front of them.

Many materials that are used to make clothing are flammable. The tragic deaths of many small children can be blamed on the highly flamma-

ble materials used to make children's nightgowns and pajamas. The clothing of a child could burn up before anyone could help him. In 1971, a law was passed ordering manufacturers to treat the fabric used in children's nightclothes with a special chemical in order to make them nonflammable. But not all clothing is treated properly, so children must be careful not to play near fires or very hot things.

Careless smokers and campers cause outdoor fires. Lighted matches, cigarettes, and campfires must always be thoroughly extinguished.

▶▶▶▶ **FIND OUT MORE** ◀◀◀◀
Fire Extinguisher; Fire Fighting; Forest Fire

◀ **A fire alarm installed in a home or workplace can help save lives. This alarm uses a** *bimetallic strip,* **made from two different metals. Fire heats up the strip, causing it to bend and complete the electric circuit, which rings the bell.**

Fire Prevention Week is observed annually during October. Many schools and communities have special clean-up projects and public information programs.

⚙ FIREWORKS

A skyrocket streaks upward into the night sky. It bursts, flinging trails of silvery fire that end in red, blue, green, and yellow stars. A few seconds later, when the stars have burned out, come several booming explosions, each marked by a flash of blinding white fire. The skyrocket is a favorite among many kinds of fireworks.

Fireworks are devices for producing colored flame and sparks, usually

◀ **The Chinese invented fireworks about 1,200 years ago. They used them mostly in religious rituals.**

The Italians were the first Europeans to use fireworks for entertainment, in about 1500. In 1572, Queen Elizabeth I of England attended a grand fireworks display at Warwick.

Wood cap

Gunpowder
and chemical
coloring

Paper cap

Quick match

Clay

Paper
casing

Gunpowder

Priming

▲ A fuse ignites the gunpowder inside a skyrocket. This produces a slow-burning explosion, giving power to the rocket.

accompanied by the noise of explosions. These things are accomplished by burning gunpowder and other chemicals. Fireworks were probably first produced by the Chinese, who also invented gunpowder—about 1,200 years ago. Because they contain explosives, fireworks are dangerous, and are illegal in many states.

The safest way to enjoy fireworks is to watch a public display. Fireworks are set off on national holidays, such as the Fourth of July. Fireworks are not toys, and playing with fireworks can be very dangerous. Like playing with guns, sooner or later, someone will be hurt.

▼ Fireworks explode in bursts of color in the sky. Much of the color comes from compounds of the metals strontium and barium. Strontium produces brilliant reds, and barium produces greens.

A *skyrocket* consists of a hollow cardboard cylinder divided into two chambers. In the rear chamber is a booster charge of gunpowder. The front chamber contains several packages of chemicals that produce the colored lights and explosions. A fuse runs from the booster charge to the chemicals and connects the chemicals together. When the fuse is lit, the gunpowder charge boosts the rocket upward. The packages of chemicals burn or explode as the fuse burns and *ignites* them (sets them afire).

A *firecracker* is a small, hollow cardboard cylinder filled with gunpowder and closed at both ends. The firecracker explodes with a sharp bang, or crack, when the gunpowder is ignited by a fuse.

A *Roman candle* is a narrow cardboard cylinder that contains several small gunpowder charges. As each charge explodes, it shoots out a brightly colored ball. A *pinwheel* swirls a shower of sparks as it spins around a center pin. A *flowerpot* shoots colored sparks upward in a pattern that looks like a plant of fire.

Not all fireworks streak upward into the air. Some are mounted on special wooden frames. Sometimes the frames hold pinwheel fireworks that twirl around. Frames may be built in shapes such as a flag, a bird, or a boat. Tiny fireworks are attached to the frames. Different colored fireworks can be used in these displays.

Fireworks are not always just for entertainment. Red fire flares, which work in a similar way to fireworks, signal railroad engineers and warn drivers of danger on highways. The skyrockets first built by the ancient Chinese were a first step toward developing the advanced rocket technology that now carries astronauts into space.

▶ ▶ ▶ ▶ **FIND OUT MORE** ◀ ◀ ◀ ◀
Explosives; Independence Day; Rocket

FIRST AID

When you help someone who has just had an accident or has suddenly become ill, you are giving first aid. But you should try to help someone only until a doctor or an ambulance arrives, and only if you know *exactly* what to do. If the wrong thing is done, the person may be in danger of being injured even more seriously.

Unless you have had special instruction in first aid in school or in a club, never try to treat an injury that is more serious than the ones mentioned here. Never try to move an injured person. Just keep the person comfortable and ask an adult for help, or call a doctor.

SHOCK. When someone is hurt very badly, he or she can easily go into *shock*. This means that his or her entire body is upset, especially the circulatory system. The symptoms of shock are pale and clammy skin, bluish lips, weak but rapid pulse, shallow breathing, and nausea. If you think someone is in shock, or might go into shock, just keep him warm and comfortable. Do not give him anything to eat or drink, as he might have a stomach injury. Call 911 or a doctor at once.

FAINTING. The victim should remain lying down. Loosen tight

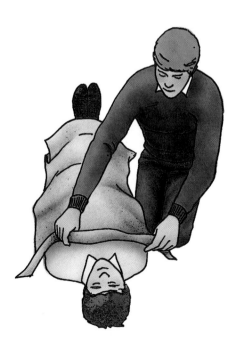

clothing and keep crowds away. If the victim vomits, roll his head to the side so he doesn't choke. Bathe his face gently with cold water. Get medical help unless recovery is prompt.

BLEEDING. Press against the bleeding area with a clean gauze pad

▼ **For bleeding, press against the wound with a clean gauze pad.**

or thick pad of clean cloth, or use your bare hand if necessary. When the bleeding stops, wash the wound with hot water and soap, rinse it, apply an antibiotic ointment, and cover with a bandage. If the bleeding does not stop within a few minutes, call an adult and go to the nearest doctor or hospital immediately. If no adult is near, call 911.

NOSEBLEED. Don't panic. Bloody noses are actually quite common. Have the person sit up and lean forward if possible. Apply pressure to the bleeding by pressing on both nostrils. Apply cold compresses to the nose and face. If the bleeding doesn't stop, insert a small, clean gauze pad (not absorbent cotton) into the nostril. Be sure to leave a bit outside the nostril so that it can be removed easily. Apply pressure again. If that fails to stop the bleeding, go to the nearest doctor or hospital.

SMALL CUTS AND SCRAPES. Clean the area thoroughly with soap and water. Check carefully to see that all dirt has been removed. Apply an

WHERE TO DISCOVER MORE

Cole, Joanna. *Cuts, Breaks, Bruises and Burns.* New York: Thomas Y. Crowell, 1985.

Elgin, Kathleen. *The Fall Down, Break a Bone, Skin Your Knee Book.* New York: Walker, 1974.

Vandenburg, Mary Lou. *Help! Emergencies That Could Happen to You, and How to Handle Them.* Minneapolis, Minnesota: Lerner Publications Co., 1975.

Many people keep a first aid kit in their home (usually the bathroom) and stock it with bandages, dressings, lotions, and scissors. This is a sensible precaution.

◀ **Do not move a person in shock. Try to keep the person warm and comfortable and do not give him or her any food or drink in case he or she has a stomach injury.**

Do not move an injured person until you know what kind of injury occurred. If there are broken bones or if there is heavy bleeding, you may harm the person more by lifting him or her.

▲ It is a good idea to keep the numbers of your poison control center and other emergency services on or near your family's telephone. Always telephone 911 quickly in an emergency.

A high percentage of accidents happen in the home. You should know where the family first aid kit is kept.

antibiotic ointment. Cover the area with a bandage to keep it clean.

POISONING. If a person swallows poison, call a poison control center for guidance, then take the person to the nearest doctor or hospital AT ONCE. Be sure to take along the container the poison was in, so the doctor will know what poison was taken and what to give. Your family should keep the poison control center number for your area on your telephone. If you do not have the number, call 911 for assistance.

FOREIGN OBJECTS IN THE EYE, NOSE, OR EAR. *In the eye:* Don't let the victim rub the eye. Ask an adult for help. An adult will gently pull down the lower lid to see if the object lies on the inner surface. If so, it can be lifted out carefully with the corner of a tissue—do not use dry cotton. If you can't see the object, the upper lid can be pulled forward and down over the lower lid, so that tears can dislodge the object. If the object can be seen on the inside of the upper lid, lift it off with the corner of a tissue. The eye should be washed well with clean, cool water. Avoid rubbing any object against the surface of the eye.

In the nose: Try to sneeze or gently blow the nose. Don't try to pull out the object. If the object doesn't come loose with gentle blowing, call a doctor.

In the ear: Don't try to dig any-

▲ For severe nosebleeds, place a small, clean gauze pad into the nostril, leaving a bit outside so that it can be removed easily. Press gently but firmly against both sides of the nose until the bleeding stops.

thing out of the ear. A few drops of warm olive oil, mineral oil, or baby oil in the ear may help, but it's best to call a doctor.

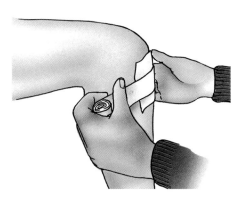

▲ Clean small cuts and scrapes carefully with soap and water; apply an antibiotic ointment, and cover with a bandage.

BURNS. Do not try to treat any burn that is more serious than a *first degree burn*—a small area on the surface of the skin that has been burned and become red. The best treatment for such burns is to hold the burned area under cold, running water. If this is not possible, put something very cold, such as an ice cube, on the burn briefly. NEVER put any kind of grease, such as salty butter or margarine, on any burn. When you take the burned area out of water, apply a dry dressing for comfort. For burns more severe than first degree, go to a doctor or a hospital.

BITES AND STINGS. Snakes, dogs, cats, insects, small rodents, and even humans can bite. Bites that break the skin may become infected, because an animal and human mouth is contaminated with bacteria. Clean the wound thoroughly, cover it, and seek medical attention.

Animals that bite may carry the *rabies* virus. If you are bitten by an animal you think is sick with rabies, go to a doctor or hospital immediately. Report any animal bite to the police so that they can catch the animal and take it to a veterinarian or dog pound. There the animal can be observed to see if it is rabid. If it is, the person it has bitten will receive a series of injections. If the animal is not rabid, the bite may just be washed, disinfected, and bandaged.

Many snakes and insects are not poisonous. Their bites need only to be cleaned with an antiseptic solution. To take the "sting" or itch out of most insect bites, apply cold water compresses and then a soothing lotion such as calamine. In the case of a bee sting, gently pull out the stinger. Don't squeeze or scratch an insect bite. Be sure to keep it clean. A person allergic to a bee sting needs special medicine immediately.

If a tick has bitten someone and it is holding on, cover it with oil, such as salad oil. This prevents the tick from breathing, and it will back out to get air. If it doesn't disengage, leave the oil in place for half an hour. Then gently remove the tick with tweezers—don't touch it. Scrub the bitten area and all areas of the body the tick has touched. Deer ticks, which cause lyme disease, are very tiny. Cover yourself completely when walking through wooded areas to avoid being bitten.

The bite or sting of a poisonous snake, spider, or scorpion will swell up and become extremely painful. A bitten person may feel like vomiting or might become unconscious. If there is a telephone nearby, call a doctor or paramedic. Have the person lie still, to prevent the poison from spreading throughout the body. If there is no telephone, get the person to a doctor or hospital immediately.

FIRST AID TRAINING. You can learn first aid from the American Red Cross. There is probably a Red Cross chapter in your city or town that gives courses in first aid. Such courses are also often given by clubs and Scout troops.

▶ ▶ ▶ ▶ **FIND OUT MORE** ◀ ◀ ◀ ◀
Artificial Respiration; Lifesaving; Poison; Poisonous Plant; Rabies; Safety

FIR TREE

SEE CONIFER

FISH

Fish were the leading form of life during the Devonian Period (the Age of Fish), which scientists believe began about 400 million years ago and lasted about 60 million years. Today there are still about 21,000 different kinds of fish. They range in size from the Philippine goby, less than half an inch (1 cm) long, to the whale shark, which grows up to 60 feet (18 m) long and weighs up to 15 tons (13.5 tonnes).

Ichthyologists (scientists who study fish) have divided them into three main groups—jawless fish, cartilaginous fish, and bony fish.

Jawless fish have suckers for mouths instead of jaws. The hagfish and lampreys are the only two kinds of jawless fish living today. The lamprey is a long, thin fish with a ring of small, sharp teeth inside its sucker mouth. It eats another fish by attaching itself to the other fish by its sucker. It scrapes a hole in the fish with its teeth and tongue, and then sucks the blood out of the fish's body. The lamprey has destroyed many important food fish, such as trout, in the Great Lakes.

Cartilaginous fish include the sharks, rays, and chimeras (ratfish). There are about 600 kinds of fish in this group. The skeletons of these fish are not made of bone, but of *cartilage*—a strong, flexible, connective tissue. The tip of your nose is made of cartilage. As you know, the cartilage of your nose can be bent and twisted, unlike your bones.

Bony fish include almost all other kinds of fish—more than 20,000 different kinds in all. Their skeletons are made of bone. Bony fish and cartilaginous fish have many differences

The fastest fish is the sailfish. One of these streamlined creatures has been timed at 68 miles per hour (109 km/hr). This is faster than any land animal.

▲ A selection of some of the earliest fish to appear on Earth. The top two creatures are types of *Ichthyosaurus,* which means "fish lizard." The bottom fish is a from the *Devonian* prehistoric era. It looks like an early type of shark with its sharp jagged jaws.

**Common shiner
6–8 in (15–20 cm)**

**American eel 2–3 ft
(60–90 cm)**

**Largemouth bass
1.5–2 ft (50–60 cm)**

**Rainbow trout 1–2 ft
(30–60 cm)**

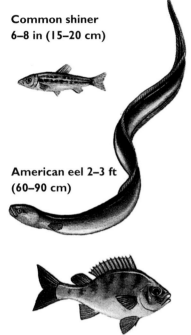

▲ North America is rich in freshwater species of fish. They live in a variety of habitats: streams, muddy rivers, and lakes.

▼ The flounder is a type of flatfish.

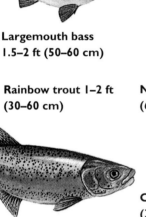

**Northern pike 2–4 ft
(60 cm–1.2 m)**

**Coho salmon 1–3 ft
(30–90 cm)**

between them. For example, most sharks and rays give birth to live off-spring. Most bony fish lay eggs.

The Bodies of Fish

Fish have a startling variety of shapes, colors, and other body features to fit their different ways of life. This variation in features is called *adaptation*. The bodies of fish that live in the open sea are usually tapered at each end. This shape helps them move swiftly through the water. They need to move quickly, because they have few places to hide from predators (animals that hunt other animals). Meat-eating fish also must swim quickly to catch other fish. Fish in the open sea are often colored bluish-green or silver. Their predators cannot spot them easily in the water.

Flatfish, such as flounder and halibut, have very flat bodies. These fish live close to the bottom of the sea and swim on their sides. Both the eyes are on the top side, and the mouth is on the bottom side. Therefore, flatfish can nibble at plants on the sandy floor while watching out for enemies that pass overhead. Many flounders are sandy colored to match their surroundings.

The anglerfish, which lives in the very deep, dark parts of the ocean, is among the oddest-looking fish. It is a fierce hunter with a huge mouth and long, sharp teeth. Its body is a dark color. The anglerfish has a *luminous* (light-giving) gland at the tip of a long, rodlike organ that rises from the end of its snout. This gland lights up to lure the anglerfish's prey to it.

Some fish have unusual weapons for self-defense. The swordfish has a long, daggerlike snout. The electric eel can give a powerful electric shock to any creature that touches it. The porcupine fish is covered with sharp spines. When frightened, it blows itself up like a balloon by swallowing water or air. Some other kinds of fish have poisonous spines.

The mouths, jaws, and teeth of fish are suited to what they eat. Those that eat fish or other animals (meat) have strong jaws and strong, sharp teeth. Plant eaters have weak teeth, or none at all. There are also some fish that eat both meat and plants.

SCALES. Nearly all fish are covered with a layer of hard plates, called *scales*, arranged in overlapping rows. A very thin layer of skin over the scales gives off a slimy substance (mucus) that coats the entire body and helps prevent infection. Scales also give protection. Some fish, such as the eel, appear to be scaleless because their scales are very tiny or are buried deep in the skin. A fish's scales grow larger as the fish grows, and scientists can tell the age of a fish by examining its scales.

GILLS. A fish has to breathe oxygen to stay alive, just as you do. But a

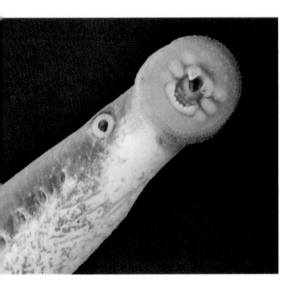

fish has *gills* instead of lungs. They are inside the fish's head, on each side of its throat. (Most fish have four gills on each side.) The gills are made of a very thin material that allows the fish's blood to come very close to the surface of the gills. The fish takes a mouthful of water and then closes its mouth, forcing the water past the gills. The oxygen in the water passes through the thin surfaces of the gills and enters the fish's blood. The water then leaves the fish's body through narrow *gill slits*, right behind the gills.

The gill slits of bony fish are covered by a thin, hard bone called a *gill cover*. The gill cover closes as water enters the mouth and opens as water passes through the gill slit. This movement of the gill cover helps pump the water past the gills. The next time you see a fish in an aquarium or a pet store, watch how it constantly swallows water and how its gill covers open and close.

AIR BLADDERS. Most fish that lived millions of years ago had not only gills but primitive lungs, which they used to store extra air. Today, only a few kinds of fish can breathe air. The lungfish breathes by rising to the surface of the water and gulping the air in through its mouth. The lungfish uses the oxygen in the air whenever it cannot get enough oxygen in its water. In hot summer weather, when the river in which it

lives dries up, the lungfish gulps in all the air it can hold. It then burrows deep into the mud at the bottom of the river. The lungfish remains inactive in the mud, in a state something like sleep, until the river fills with water again.

The lungs of most kinds of bony fish gradually changed over the centuries into a balloonlike organ called an *air bladder,* or *swim bladder.* This organ helps a fish to stay motionless without either rising or sinking. The air bladder fills up with some of the oxygen dissolved in the fish's blood. This keeps the fish from sinking. Some fish gulp air at the surface of the water to fill their air bladders. Herring, salmon, pike, and catfish do this.

◄ **A living example of a jawless fish—a river lamprey. Its several gills are clearly visible at its side.**

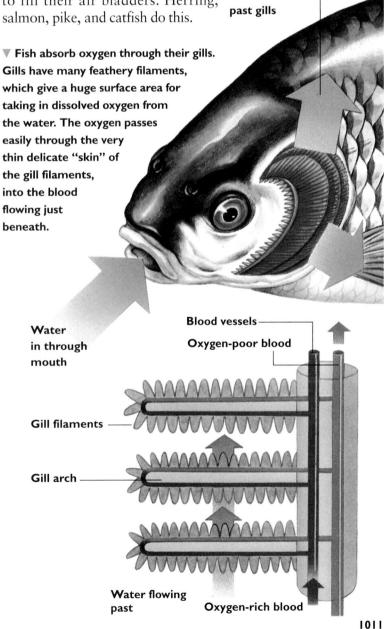

▼ **Fish absorb oxygen through their gills. Gills have many feathery filaments, which give a huge surface area for taking in dissolved oxygen from the water. The oxygen passes easily through the very thin delicate "skin" of the gill filaments, into the blood flowing just beneath.**

Water out past gills

Water in through mouth

Blood vessels

Oxygen-poor blood

Gill filaments

Gill arch

Water flowing past

Oxygen-rich blood

▶ **The different parts of a fish, illustrated here in this cutaway picture.**

▼ **A devilfish, the largest type of flying fish. It gets its name from the hornlike flaps on its head. The horns scoop food into its mouth. The fins of this fish can be more than 20 feet (6 m) across, and it can weigh up to 4,400 lbs. (2,000 kg).**

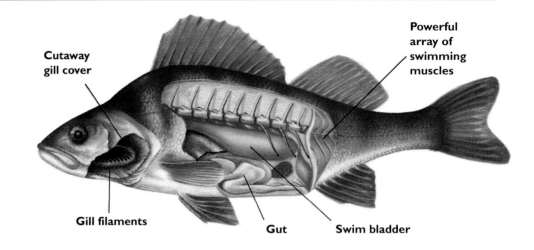

Cutaway gill cover

Powerful array of swimming muscles

Gill filaments

Gut

Swim bladder

▼ **A fish swims by flexing its body and tail fins from side to side. It does this, in a flowing movement, by alternately contracting the muscles on each side of its body.**

FINS. Fins help a fish to swim. A few fish, such as the seahorse and the eel, have only one fin. But most other fish have several fins. A fish swims by waving its body and a tail fin (*caudal* fin) back and forth. This motion pushes the fish forward. The fins near the tail fin, the *dorsal* fin on top and the *anal* fin on the bottom, help the fish keep its balance. On the bottom near the head are two *pelvic* fins that are used for slow swimming. Two *pectoral* fins, at the sides just behind the head, help the fish change direction or slow down as it swims. The pectoral fins stick out from either side of the fish's body. Fish with large pectoral fins can change direction suddenly and can dart forward or backward.

Flying fish have very long pectoral fins. A flying fish first swims to the surface of the water. It gathers speed by waving its caudal fin back and forth very quickly. When the fish is moving at top speed, it stretches out its pectoral fins and glides into the air. Most flying fish stay in the air only a few seconds, which is long enough for them to escape their enemies. The longest a flying fish has been known

Sharks and rays do not have air bladders at all. These fish cannot remain motionless in the water as bony fish can. They begin to sink the minute they stop swimming.

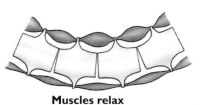

Muscles relax

Muscles contract

Muscles contract

Muscles relax

to glide through the air is 42 seconds. On a long glide, the flying fish may travel 1,200 feet (375 m).

The walking perch, which lives in Asia and Australia, uses its pectoral and tail fins to walk on land. It does this at night to travel from one stream or pond to another. The walking perch has long spines on its gill

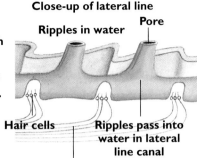

A fish's lateral line, its special sense organ that detects vibrations, consists of a groove or tube that runs along each side of the body and contains sensitive hairs. Water movements rock the hairs and generate nerve signals to the brain.

Close-up of lateral line
Ripples in water
Pore
Hair cells
Ripples pass into water in lateral line canal
Nerves to brain

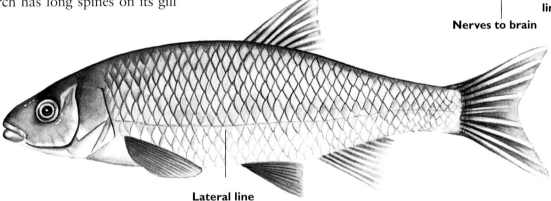

Lateral line

cover that help it cling to the ground as it walks along.

Rays and skates have developed very long pectoral fins. Skin has grown from the fins along the sides of the body almost to the tail fins. Rays and skates swim by waving their pectoral fins. Some kinds of rays move their pectoral fins the same way that birds flap their wings.

SENSES. Most fish can smell and taste very well. They smell through their nostrils and taste through their skin, as well as their mouths. The senses of sight and hearing are keen in

many fish. You cannot see a fish's ears, because they are deep inside its head. Sound waves reach the ears through the bone of the skull. A fish's eyes are specially adapted for seeing under water. The unusual "four eyed" fish of Central and South America can see in air and in water at the same time. Each of its eyes has a band of skin that divides the pupil in two. This fish swims close to the surface of the water when feeding, so that its upper pupils can look for bits of food floating on top of the water. Fish that live in dark caves or deep in the sea, where there is no light, have very poor eyesight. Some are blind.

Fish also have a special sense organ, called the *lateral line organ*. It is a hollow tube that runs along both sides of the fish's body just under the skin. This organ is especially sensitive to vibrations, or movements, in the water. It lets the fish know what is going on around it, even if it does not see, hear, or smell anything. For example, if you are fishing for trout, your footsteps along the bank of a stream will produce vibrations in the water. The trout will sense these vibrations through its lateral line organ and will swim away.

◄ A thornback ray. Rays are related to sharks and, like them, they have cartilaginous skeletons. Rays have flattened bodies, with the mouth, nostrils, and gill openings on their underside and the eyes on the back. Their strange shape is adapted to life on the seabed.

QUIZ

1. Name the three main groups of fish.
2. What is the name for scientists who study fish?
3. How many gills do most fish have?
4. What does a fish's air bladder do?
5. How many fins do most fish have?

(Answers on page 1024)

Reproduction

Most female fish *spawn,* or lay eggs. The male fish swim among the eggs, discharging their sperm into the water to fertilize the eggs. The fertilized eggs roll in the current or catch in weeds. The young fish that hatch feed on food particles that float on the surface of the water.

Female fish usually lay an enormous number of eggs. The female cod lays seven million eggs at one time. But very few of these eggs will ever hatch. Most are eaten by fish and other sea animals. Many of the young fish that do hatch are eaten by other creatures, too.

Some kinds of ocean fish spawn on the floor of the sea. These fish usually lay a smaller number of eggs. The eggs have a sticky surface and remain where they have been laid. Fish such as the stickleback even build a nest of plants in which the female fish can lay her eggs. The male stickleback guards the eggs until they hatch. Seahorse females place their eggs in a pouch on the male's belly. The male seahorse fertilizes the eggs and cares for them until they hatch.

Some fish migrate, or travel very long distances, to breed and spawn. The Pacific salmon is hatched in streams in the western parts of Canada and the United States. The young salmon then travel down these streams to the Pacific Ocean to grow. When the time comes for the females to spawn, they and the male salmon travel back to the streams where they

◀ Seahorses are bony fish that swim in an upright position. They curl their tails around plants, such as seaweeds, when they want to cling to something. During courtship, the female seahorse places her eggs into a special pouch on the male's belly to be fertilized. They remain there until they hatch.

▼ A salmon lays its eggs in the upper parts of rivers, even though it spends much of its life in the sea. Baby salmon, called alevin, hatch with their food supply in a special pouch.

larvae after hatching

were hatched. There the female salmon deposits her eggs and the male salmon fertilizes them. The adult salmon then die.

▶ ▶ ▶ ▶ **FIND OUT MORE** ◀ ◀ ◀ ◀
Fishing see Fishing; Fishing Industry
Habitat see Marine Life; Pond Life; Water Pollution
Habits and Features see Egg; Migration; Protective Coloring; Reproduction; Respiration; Teeth
Kinds of Fish see Blindfish; Seahorse; Sharks And Rays
Pets see Aquarium; Pet

FISHING

Fishing is a popular and relaxing way for people of all ages to spend their spare time. People who catch their own fish enjoy eating them, too. But a good sportsman never catches more fish than he or she can use, and always throws back any fish that have not grown to their proper size.

Methods of Fishing

The equipment that fishermen use to catch fish is called *tackle.* The kind of tackle and the fishing method they use depend on where they are fishing and what kind of fish they want to catch. *Still fishing* is the simplest method and is probably the most common way of catching freshwater fish such as catfish, sunfish, yellow perch, and white bass. Still-fishing needs little equipment—only a fishing rod or maybe just a long pole. A fishing *line*—a piece of cotton or nylon thread—is tied to the end of the rod. A fishing *hook,* usually made of stout steel wire, is tied to the other end of the line. Fishermen attach some *bait* to their hooks. The

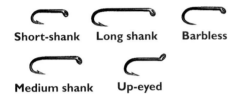

Short-shank   Long shank   Barbless

Medium shank   Up-eyed

▲ **"Up-eyed" and "down-eyed" hooks are commonly used for fly casting.**

bait may be an earthworm, frog, crayfish, grasshopper, or some other small animal that fish eat. Fishermen simply drop their baited hooks into the water and wait for fish to "bite." When a fish seizes the bait, the hook will catch in its mouth. Some fish swallow the hook.

Fishermen also use *sinkers* and *floats.* The sinker is a piece of lead tied near the hook. It keeps the bait from floating to the surface of the water. The float is a piece of cork or wood attached to the line. It floats on the surface of the water and bobs up and down when a fish takes the bait in its mouth and starts to tug on the hook. The bob may be no more than just a circle of ripples moving out from the float, but it is enough for fishermen to know that something is nibbling at the bait. Fishermen jerk their rods sharply upward to "set" the hook in the fish's mouth so that the fish cannot escape.

CASTING. A more complicated way of fishing, called *casting,* is popular for both saltwater and freshwater fishing. When fishermen *cast* their lines, they throw the hook far across the water by raising the rod over the shoulder and then whipping it forward. Fishermen need special reels and rods to cast for fish. For *spin casting,* their reel consists of a spool of very thin strong nylon line that is enclosed in a cap. When fishermen cast, they push a button to release the line. They turn a small crank on the reel to rewind the line so that they can make another cast.

▲ **Fishing is a sport that can be enjoyed by people of all ages. The man here is pulling in his catch with the help of a fishing net.**

◄ **Fishing on Lake Winnipesaukee, New Hampshire. The man and child seen here, are putting bait onto their fishing hooks, before they start to fish.**

Wet fly

Dry fly

Lure

▲ **Three kinds of flies used for fly casting: Wet flies have wings that slope back over the hook shank; dry flies have sparse, light wings; and lures are usually used underwater.**

Fish supply about 12 percent of the protein needed to feed a growing world population. The total yearly catch of fish from the world's oceans is almost 70 million tons (71 million metric tons).

The *bait-casting* rod is shorter and stiffer than a spin-casting rod. The reel has a wide spool that lies across the width of the rod. When fishermen make a cast with a bait caster, the reel spins as the line unwinds from it. Fishermen rewind their lines by turning a crank on the reel.

Instead of using live bait, fishermen can use *lures* or *plugs* for bait casting or spin casting. The lure looks like a minnow (small fish) or other live bait. It is usually made of metal or plastic and is heavy enough to fly long distances through the air when properly cast with a rod. Fishermen move their rods about as they reel in their lines to make the lure look like a live fish swimming in the water. They may use a sinker and float with the lure to make the lure look like a fish swimming deep in the water.

Fly casting is fishing with a fly as bait to attract fish. The fly is made of colored pieces of thread and feathers fastened together to look like a small insect. The fly hides the hook. The hook is fastened to a long *leader* made of clear nylon, which is invisible in the water. Fly casting is a common method of catching trout.

Surf casting is a special technique of saltwater fishing. Fishermen may wade into the ocean from the shore, or they may cast from a pier or some rocks that jut out from the water. If they fish from the shore, they use a special long rod with a long line, so that they can cast their bait or lure over the waves. Saltwater fishermen especially like to fish this way for sea bass. Sea bass is different from the bass swimming in fresh water. The jewfish is one of many kinds of sea bass. It can weigh up to 700 lbs. (320 kg).

TROLLING. Fishing from a moving boat is called *trolling*. Fishermen throw their lines over the side of their boat and let the lure or plug trail through the water as the boat moves slowly along. This is the usual method for deep-sea fishing. Deep-sea anglers fish for tuna, marlin,

▲ **Ice fishing through a hole cut in the ice is common in winter on frozen lakes and frozen Arctic seas.**

swordfish, and sailfish. Some of these fish weigh as much as several hundred pounds. The anglers use a very heavy fishing rod and a strong line. They sit in special chairs on the rear of the fishing launch and fasten a safety belt across the waist to prevent the fish from pulling them overboard. It may take hours to tire one of these big fish out and finally bring it on board.

All fish have different living habits. They prefer different kinds of food, and they live in different kinds of streams and lakes. Good fishermen study the habits of the fish they want to catch and learn where to find them. Serious fishermen are called anglers. They enjoy using their skill to catch fish that are hard to catch and put up a good fight. Some anglers are so proud of their skill that they hold casting contests in empty fields just to see which angler has the most control. A good angler can cast into a small target 300 feet (90 m) away.

▶ ▶ ▶ ▶ **FIND OUT MORE** ◀ ◀ ◀ ◀
Fish; Fishing industry

FISHING INDUSTRY

Fish and shellfish are very nutritious foods. They are excellent sources of protein and of many vitamins and minerals that people need to stay healthy. Parts of fish can be made into fertilizer; glue; feed for chickens, cats, and livestock; and many other things. Because fish are such a useful product, the catching and preparation of great quantities of fish has become one of the world's most important industries. People who live close to the sea and who do not have enough farmland to grow all the food they need are particularly great fish eaters. Japan and Russia are the world's leading fishing countries. China, the United States, Chile, Norway, Canada, and Spain also have large fishing industries.

Millions of people are employed in these and other countries not only to catch fish but also to prepare them. Some fish are sold fresh or frozen.

Fish may also be cooked before it is frozen, so that it just needs to be heated before eating. Many kinds of fish are canned, smoked, or salted.

The parts of fish that are not eaten—such as the heads, fins, bones, and internal organs—are made into fertilizers and animal feed. The livers of some fish are rich in vitamins A and D. Many people take cod-liver oil to get these vitamins. Oils from the bodies of other fish are used to make candles, soap, paint, and printer's ink. Some shoes are made from sharkskin. A special fish organ

American commercial fishing takes place off the eastern, southern, and western coasts and in the Great Lakes. Alaska is the leading fishing state, followed by Louisiana and Virginia.

▼ Some fishing methods and the fish they catch. Fish are caught by their gills in gill nets; in long-line fishing, baited hooks are attached to a long line. A purse seine net is drawn around a school of fish; lobsters are snared in traps. The otter trawl net is dragged over the seabed, trapping fish that live at the bottom of the sea.

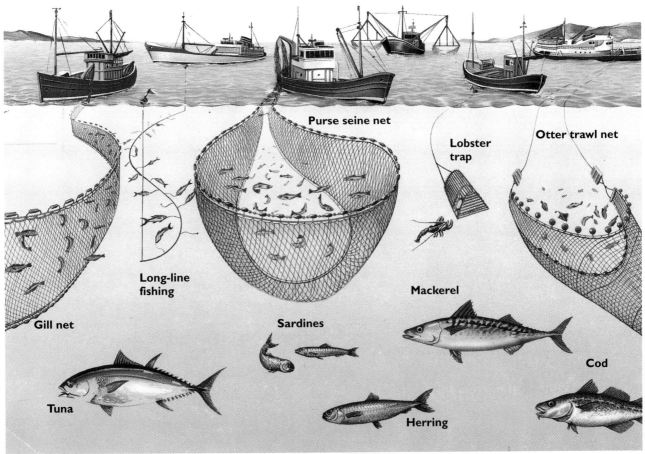

▶ This diagram shows the layout of a typical freezer trawler capable of quick-freezing hundreds of tons of fish at sea.

Radar

Factory decks

Bridge

Winch

Crew's quarters

Storeroom

Engine room   Fuel tanks   Stabilization tanks   Cold storage

▲ In one traditional method of fishing, the people in eastern Asia use cormorants (a variety of fish-eating seabird) to catch the fish for them. They then pick the fish up with nets.

called the air bladder produces *isinglass,* a gelatin used in jellies, glue, and cement.

Cod, haddock, mackerel, herring, halibut, salmon, tuna, ocean perch, flounder, and sardines are among the most popular fish for eating. More than twice as many sardines and pilchards are caught each year than any other kind of fish. Commercial fishermen also catch *shellfish,* such as shrimps, clams, oysters, lobsters, scallops, and crabs. All of these fish and shellfish are caught in oceans, although salmon can also be caught in freshwater lakes and rivers. Some other freshwater food fish are trout, catfish, pike, and perch. The Great Lakes are an important source of these for the United States and Canada.

Commercial Fishing Methods

Commercial fishermen use special fishing methods for catching large amounts of fish. Cod are caught with lines and baited hooks by fishermen on the Grand Banks. The Grand Banks are shallow places in the Atlantic Ocean off the coast of Newfoundland. Cod live in cold water, and conditions are just right for them on the Grand Banks. Fishermen come from the United States, Canada, Europe, and Russia to fish for cod there. They use lines and hooks to catch cod because the ocean floor is rocky, and nets would tear.

Many years ago, fishermen in America used to catch cod from small rowboats called *dories.* The

fishermen traveled to the Grand Banks in large sailing schooners, but each fisherman would go off in his own dory every morning with a supply of fishing lines, floats, and bait. He would drop his fishing line, with its baited hook, into the water and tie a float to the other end of the line to keep from losing it. Whenever a cod was hooked, the fisherman pulled the fish into his dory. He rowed back to his schooner when his dory was full of fish. The fish were then cleaned and packed away in salt, which kept the fish from spoiling. The fishermen worked hard from sunrise to sunset. They would stay on the Grand Banks until their schooners were full of fish.

Commercial fishermen still use hooks and lines to catch fish. But today they tie the fishing lines to a long rope. The rope is held in the water by buoys. It may be several miles long and may have as many as 5,000 fishing lines hanging down from it.

Nets are most commonly used in commercial fishing, because they can gather in a large school of fish in a single sweep. One type of net is the bag-shaped *otter trawl.* It is used to catch shrimps, crabs, and fish that live near the bottom of the sea, such as flounder. The fishermen throw the otter trawl over the rear of their ship, called a *trawler.* Strong ropes are fastened to the sides of the net. Wheels on the bottom of the net keep the net from catching on any rocks on the ocean floor. Floats on the top hold the net open so fish can swim into it. Pieces of wood are fastened to each side of the net. These pieces of wood pull the open side of the net wide apart as the trawler moves through the water.

When the fishermen think the net is full of fish, they pull it out of the water and dump the fish onto the deck of the trawler. The fish are packed away in crushed ice, so that they stay fresh until the ship reaches port again. A large trawler might stay at sea for three weeks or more. Some modern trawlers have large freezers on board. The fish are packed in containers and frozen solid just after they are caught. They taste fresh when they are eaten later.

A *gill* net is used for catching fish that swim close to the surface. This net is stretched out in the water like a fence. The bottom of the net sinks deep into the water, while the top is held up by floats. Sometimes these nets are a mile long. The openings in the gill nets are just large enough for fish to stick their heads through. Their gill covers get stuck in the net when they try to back out. The fishermen then pull the net out of the water and empty the fish into their boat. Gill nets with openings of different sizes are used for catching different kinds of fish.

Fish that are caught with gill nets include herrings, sardines, and anchovies. They are caught mainly in the Atlantic Ocean off the coast of Europe. The sardine and anchovy fishermen have canning equipment on board their fishing vessels. The fish are cleaned and packed in cans as soon as they are caught. The cans are then cooked in hot water to kill any bacteria that might spoil the fish. Sardines and anchovies are usually packed in oil, because bacteria cannot live in oil. Herrings are sometimes salted or smoked.

▶▶▶▶ **FIND OUT MORE** ◀◀◀◀
Fish; Fishing; Food Processing

FIVE NATIONS

Five strong tribes of the Iroquois people, who lived in what is now the state of New York, joined together in a league called the Five Nations about 1570. They were the Seneca, Cayuga, Onondaga, Oneida, and Mohawk tribes. Two Mohawk Native Americans, Deganawida, a Huron, and Hiawatha, founded the league to stop the tribes from warring with each other. The league became the most powerful Native American organization in North America.

▲ **A fisherman winching in a net full of fish on a commercial fishing trawler. Commercial fishermen employ various methods to catch large amounts of fish.**

▼ **Hiawatha, the Mohawk tribe leader, was able to convince other tribes in the Iroquois league to unite in 1570 against the Algonquians.**

▲ Hendrick, a chief of the Mohawk tribe, which was part of the Five Nations, seen here urging his men on to victory during the French and Indian Wars.

▼ The flag of the United Kingdom is made up of three flags: the Irish flag (second); the Scottish flag (third); and the English flag (bottom).

The council of the Five Nations met every summer. The 50 members of the council, called *sachems,* who were leaders of their tribes, discussed matters with other leaders of the tribes and then voted. Each tribe had one vote. But a decision could not be reached until all the sachems agreed. Long debates were often held before they could come to an agreement.

The Five Nations were powerful and well organized by the time European colonists came to America. An Iroquois tribe called the Tuscarora came from North Carolina to New York and joined the league in 1722. The league then became known as the Six Nations. The British later became allied with the Six Nations. With Iroquois help, the British won the French and Indian War (1754–1763), which led to the end of French rule in North America.

▶▶▶▶ **FIND OUT MORE** ◀◀◀◀
French and Indian War; Iroquois; Native Americans

FLAG

Flags are symbols. They are only patterned pieces of cloth. But they can stand for a whole country, a state, or an important person. That is why Americans say:

"I pledge allegiance to the flag of the United States of America and to the Republic for which it stands..."

Every independent country in the world has its own flag. Parts of countries and cities also have flags. Each U.S. state has its own flag. So do the provinces and territories of Canada. The United Nations has a special flag. Organizations such as the Boy Scouts and the Girl Scouts have flags. Important offices such as those of the President and the Secretary of State have flags, too.

Many flags have interesting stories behind them. It is said that the flag

of Austria was invented by an Austrian duke. He had lost his regular flags in battle, so he decided to use his tunic (a loose-fitting garment) as a flag. The tunic was red with blood from the battle. But it had a white stripe across it where the duke's belt had covered it. Because of this the Austrian flag is now red with a horizontal white stripe.

A group of Aztec people in the 1100s watched as an eagle perched on a cactus and ate a snake. They believed this was a special sign and they founded a town on the spot. The Aztec town later became Mexico City. So Mexico's flag has a picture of an eagle eating a snake.

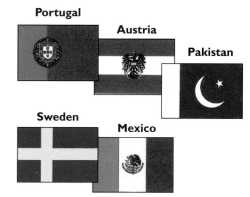

Portugal
Austria
Pakistan
Sweden
Mexico

▲ A selection of flags from different countries in the world.

Many countries have special national symbols on their flags. Lebanon has a picture of one of its famous cedars. Portugal has a picture of a navigation instrument in honor of the famous Portuguese explorers.

Religious symbols appear on many flags. Turkey, Pakistan, Tunisia, and several other Arab countries have the crescent and star of Islam on their flags. The Mongolian flag has a combination of Buddhist symbols. The flag of Israel has the six-pointed star of David, a symbol of Judaism.

Many European flags have crosses on them. The Scandinavian countries of Denmark, Norway, Sweden, and Finland all have flags with crosses in the same position but of different

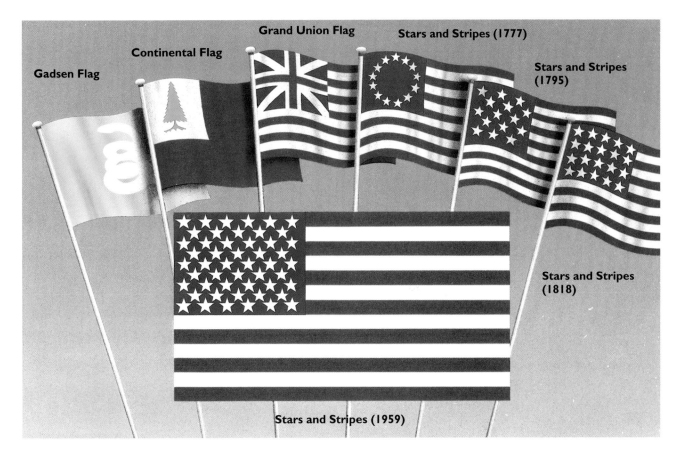

Gadsen Flag

Continental Flag

Grand Union Flag

Stars and Stripes (1777)

Stars and Stripes (1795)

Stars and Stripes (1818)

Stars and Stripes (1959)

color combinations. The Grand Union flag is the flag of the United Kingdom (Great Britain and Northern Ireland). It is a combination of three different crosses that appeared on the flags of England, Scotland, and Ireland. England's flag had the cross of Saint George, which is a horizontal red cross on a white background. Scotland's flag had the cross of Saint Andrew—a diagonal white cross (like an X) on a background of blue. And Ireland had the cross of Saint Patrick—a diagonal red cross on a white background.

The Stars and Stripes
Many different flags were flown during the Revolutionary War. One of them showed a pine tree. Others showed a rattlesnake with the words "Don't Tread on Me." This was a warning to the British to stop interfering in the life of the colonies. The Grand Union flag was also used. Its *canton*, which is the rectangular part of the flag on the upper left side, showed the crosses of Saint George

and Saint Andrew. The rest of the flag had 13 stripes of red and white.

The Continental Congress passed a resolution on June 14, 1777, "That the United States flag be thirteen stripes, alternate red and white, that the Union [canton] be thirteen stars, white in a blue field representing a new constellation." The new flag was called the Stars and Stripes. Much mystery surrounds its creation. According to legend, Betsy Ross, who lived in Philadelphia, made the first American flag. The resolution of 1777 did not say how the stars should be arranged. Most early flags had the stars in a circle. But some had them in horizontal lines. Two new states had been formed by 1795, and Congress brought the number of stars and stripes up to 15. But it was later decided that if a new stripe was added for each new state, it would ruin the flag design. So Congress passed a law in 1818 returning the flag to its original 13 stripes. The law also said that a new star would be added for each new state.

▲ The United States flag, the "Stars and Stripes," has changed many times, but the basic elements have remained the same.

▼ In the Middle Ages every prince and nobleman had his own flag or banner that would be carried proudly into battle.

▲ The Salvation Army flag—a symbol of the religious and charitable organization, founded in England in 1865 by the Methodist minister William Booth.

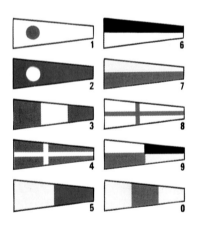

International signal flags used at sea include a flag for each letter of the alphabet as well as the numerals one to ten shown above These signal flags appeared in the eighteenth century as a means of sending messages.

Rules for Displaying the Flag

Because the flag is a symbol of the United States, it should be treated with respect at all times. Many rules tell how the flag is to be treated. Here are some of the important ones. 1. When you are saluting the flag or saying the pledge of allegiance, stand up straight with your right hand over your heart. People in uniform should give military salutes. If you are watching a parade and a flag is carried past you, salute it the moment it passes. 2. The flag should be displayed properly and stored carefully so that there is little chance of it becoming torn or dirty. The flag should never touch anything beneath it, such as the ground, the floor, water, or merchandise. It should not be used in an advertisement or as part of a costume. When a flag has become very torn or dirty, it should be destroyed in a dignified way, preferably by burning it or burying it. 3. The flag should be displayed every day in good weather. It is usually displayed from sunrise to sunset but can be flown at night. When flown at night, the flag should be spotlighted. It is customarily displayed on national holidays and other special days, such as Memorial Day and the day of the Presidential Inauguration.

Other Uses for Flags

Some flag signals have international meanings. A flag hung at half mast (halfway up the flagpole) is a sign of *mourning* (honor for the dead). A flag hung upside down means distress. A green flag means a wrecked ship. A white flag is a sign of surrender in battle or of truce. A red flag means danger. An international code uses signal flags to represent different letters, words, and numbers. Using this code, ships can send messages back and forth. Each flag stands for one letter of the alphabet. Extra flags or pennants stand for the numerals zero to nine. Ships interpret the messages by means of a code book that explains the code in nine languages—English, French, German, Italian, Spanish, Russian, Norwegian, Greek, and Japanese. Some of the flags from the code can be used singly for certain messages. For example, the flags P, Y, and U used together wish another ship a good voyage.

▶▶▶▶ **FIND OUT MORE** ◀◀◀◀
Ross, Betsy; Signal

FLAX

SEE PLANT PRODUCTS

FLEMING, SIR ALEXANDER (1881–1955)

Alexander Fleming was a British *bacteriologist* (a scientist who studies bacteria). He discovered the lifesaving power of the mold called penicillin.

Fleming was born on a Scottish farm. He graduated with honors from St. Mary's Hospital Medical School of the University of London in 1908. Fleming served with the Royal Army Medical Corps in France during World War I. He became interested in *septic*, or infected, wounds during his work as an army doctor. In 1922, he discovered that egg whites, human tears, and human tissues all contain the same antiseptic, or germ-killer. He named it *lysozyme*.

In 1928, Fleming noticed clear spots in some colonies of bacteria he was growing in his laboratory. He realized that something had killed the bacteria in these spots. He found that the spots contained a mold—a fungus growth—called *Penicillium notatum*. He then discovered that the mold contained a substance that killed the bacteria. He named this substance *penicillin*. He was able to take a little penicillin from the fungus mold. This was the first antibiotic and by far the most powerful germ-killer known at that time.

For his discovery of penicillin, Dr. Fleming shared the 1945 Nobel Prize in medicine with Howard W. Florey and Ernest B. Chain, the doctors who found a way to produce penicillin in large quantities.

▶ ▶ ▶ ▶ **FIND OUT MORE** ◀ ◀ ◀ ◀
Antibiotic; Bacteria; Drug; Fungus; Nobel Prize

FLIGHTLESS BIRDS

Four of the world's largest birds are flightless species (kinds). They are unable to fly because they do not have a *keel*. A keel is a bony ridge connected to the breast bone to which the chest muscles of flying birds are attached, giving them the power to keep a bird in the air. The most familiar of the flightless birds is undoubtedly the *ostrich*, the largest living bird. A male ostrich may weigh more than 300 pounds (135 kg) and be 8 feet (2.5 m) tall. The ostrich differs from all other birds by having two toes on each foot rather than three or four.

Ostriches live in small groups on the plains and deserts of Africa. On flat land they can run at 40 miles

(65 km) an hour. Their speed and their extra-sharp sight usually help them escape their enemies—lions and men. A cornered ostrich can't fly away from an enemy but can give it a vicious kick. Ostriches mainly eat plants but will also eat lizards and turtles when they can catch them.

A female ostrich lays 12 to 16 eggs. They are the largest eggs of any living bird and weigh about 3 pounds (1.5 kg) each. The male and the female birds share the task of sitting on the eggs until they hatch, in about six weeks. Newborn ostriches are about a foot (30 cm) tall.

Another flightless bird is the *cassowary* of northern Australia and nearby islands. The largest of these birds stands nearly 4 feet (1.2 m) high and weighs more than 100 pounds (45 kg). Cassowaries have strong legs and long, sharp claws. On top of the head is a bony comb, a crownlike growth used to butt through branches and vines. Cassowaries generally live in forests. They eat fruits, herbs, and various small animals.

The third of these flightless birds, the *emu*, also lives in Australia. Emus travel in small groups, feeding on plants and fruits as they move about. Emus weigh about 100 pounds (45 kg), stand more than 5 feet (1.5 m) tall, and can run about 30 miles (50 km) an hour. They destroy crops and may knock down sheep fences. They cause much trouble for Australian farmers and ranchers. A female emu

▲ **Sir Alexander Fleming, the British bacteriologist who discovered the life-saving antibiotic penicillin.**

◀ **An ostrich, the largest living bird. Ostriches roam in herds on the African plains and deserts, led by a male. They eat almost anything they can find.**

◀ **The emu is Australia's biggest bird. Emus roam around in small flocks, mainly on grasslands. They are becoming rare, but are being bred successfully in captivity.**

lays as many as a dozen eggs in a grass nest. Then the male sits on the eggs until they hatch.

A fourth flightless bird is the *rhea*, a South American bird. Rheas are often called "South American ostriches," but this name is incorrect. Rheas stand just under 5 feet (1.5 m) tall. They weigh about 50

◀ **The rhea lives on the plains of South America. It is a fast and agile runner.**

◀ **Kiwis (bottom left) are shy birds that live in forests. They sleep by day and hunt at night. Penguins live at the South Pole.**

pounds (23 kg). Rheas make their homes near water where they can swim and bathe. About 30 birds live together, eating insects, roots, and leaves. Several females lay their eggs in one nest, which a male forms by scraping a hole in the ground. The male hatches the eggs—as many as 60.

Several smaller birds are also flightless. The best known of these is the chicken-sized kiwi of New Zealand forests. A kiwi's wings are only 2 inches (5 cm) long. Kiwis have such strong legs, however, that these birds are said to be able to run faster than people can. They walk around at night, feeding on berries, leaves, insects, and worms.

Other flightless birds include two kinds of rails, a grebe, and penguins.

▶▶▶▶ **FIND OUT MORE** ◀◀◀◀
Bird; Penguin

QUIZ ANSWERS

English History quiz, page 925
1. The Romans settled in Britain first, from about 55 B.C. to about A.D. 400. The Vikings invaded around A.D. 700.
2. The Normans introduced the feudal system into English society. This system lasted for about 200 years.
3. King John was forced to sign the Magna Carta in 1215.
4. The House of Lancaster and the House of York were the two opposing sides in the Wars of the Roses.
5. The longest reigning British monarch was Queen Victoria, who held the throne for 64 years (1837–1901).
6. England, Scotland, Wales, and Northern Ireland make up the United Kingdom.

Europe quiz, page 948
1. The idea of democracy began in Europe in the ancient city of Athens, Greece.
2. There are hundreds of languages and dialects throughout Europe. Three of these are: English, Swedish and Polish.
3. The fourth-smallest European country (in size) is Liechtenstein. The fourth-smallest in population is a tie between Monaco and Liechtenstein. The largest nation in size and population is Russia.
4. The Ural Mountains separate Europe from Asia.
5. The 40-degree latitudinal line from Rome, Italy, west runs through Philadelphia on the East Coast of the U.S.

Evolution quiz, page 956
1. No. He believed that animals could choose to change themselves physically to adapt to new needs. In reality, the process is purely accidental. Slight variations occur by chance.

2. The earliest known ancestor of the camel first appeared in North America. It was about the size of a jackrabbit.
3. The giraffe born with the longer neck will probably live longest and produce more offspring. He will be able to reach more food, and will therefore be healthier, stronger, and probably faster so that he will be able to escape from predators.
4. Genetic mutations can be either good or bad. A mutation that makes someone ill or causes him or her to die at a very young age is obviously bad. However, a mutation can also improve the person or animal who is born with it.
5. In all living cells there are threads of matter called chromosomes. These contain the nucleic acid called DNA. DNA is arranged in a number of very small units called genes. Genes determine individual characteristics.

Fish quiz, page 1014
1. The three main groups of fish are: jawless fish, cartilaginous fish, and bony fish.
2. Scientists who study fish are called *ichthyologists*. "Ichthy" means fish in the ancient Latin language (which got the word from the ancient Greek *ichthys*).
3. Most fish have four gills on each side of their bodies.
4. A fish's air bladder was once its lungs. The air bladder fills up with oxygen and helps the fish keep its place underwater and keep from sinking.
5. Most fish have seven fins: the caudal (tail) fin, the dorsal and anal fins (near the caudal), two pelvic fins, and two pectoral fins.